THE BUSINESS OF KAYFABE

THE BUSINESS OF KAYFABE

TURNING WRESTLERS' SECRETS INTO A MILLION DOLLARS

BY SEAN OLIVER

Also by the author:

<u>Non-fiction</u>
Kayfabe
Fathers' Blood

<u>Fiction</u>
Sophie's Journal

Cover photo and rear photo by Mia Oliver.

ISBN-13: 9781795165808

www.seanoliverbooks.com

For Matt and Nicky. World champions.

CONTENTS

Introduction

IT DOESN'T MAKE a damn bit of difference how good you are at business, directing, or talent relations. Wrestlers, and the wrestling business, will consistently find ways to circumvent your talents and abilities. The best-laid plans are subject to turn on their heads, due to the nature of this minefield industry. You'll eventually question whether you can get anything at all done without a migraine.

And Jim Powers was making my head pound like a Tommy Lee drum solo.

The weekend was all set and despite plans to start production on a brand new series, the schedule was easy-breezy.

Several months prior, we were breaking down the set of

Breaking Kayfabe with Scott "Raven" Levy, when Vince Russo called me. Vince is the controversial former writer for WWE, WCW, and TNA and he'd just started a podcast. On it, he was recapping past episodes of wrestling TV for which he wrote and those recaps of classic WWE RAW episodes were doing great downloads for him. He thought of his old pal in New Jersey—the guy that scooped him up after the implosion of his stint at TNA and set him on his feet again with our brilliant *YouShoot: LIVE!*—and pitched me a show that he envisioned as the video compliment to the audio podcast.

With some tweaking, we came up with *Vince Russo's Attitude,* wherein Vince would host and sit with a member of the WWE roster from the era when Vince was writing its TV. We knew his trips down memory lane would be fun as he sat with the guys and gals from the era that saved wrestling's biggest federation from certain doom at the hands of plumbers, pig farmers, and hockey goons in their ring. We would fly him out and shoot a few episodes of the show to pilot.

We booked the first two guests—Ken Shamrock and Terri Runnels. After slating the new show for release and having Anthony research Vince's time writing for both Ken and Terri, we sent it all to Vince and put it all on the shooting schedule for a Friday and Saturday.

Then I got a call from a talent booker that we sometimes used named Nick, who offered us Paul Roma for one of our shows. I'd heard Paul on shows before and knew him to be outspoken so I made an offer for him to appear on our show *Breaking Kayfabe.* I thought we could talk to Paul about his time in WWE and his issues with them, as well as the not-so-friendly break-up with his Young Stallions tag team partner Jim Powers.

Nick called me and said Paul rejected the offer out of hand, solely on the money. I forget the words exactly and I don't want to put any in Paul's mouth, but I know I was pissed because it was dismissive. Apparently the money offer offended the former member of the Four Horsemen.

Well, that was that. Mr. Roma and I were clearly on separate sides of the universe regarding his drawing power in the wrestling aftermarket. I wasn't moving on the money. I thanked Nick for reaching out and got to work coordinating flights for Terri and Vince so they could land in Newark at roughly the same time. Then Nick called me again.

"Hey since it didn't work out with Paul," he began, "how about booking Jim Powers for the other side of that story?" I was intrigued. Jim was another very honest interview guest who I'd never worked with before. Well, unless you count his spontaneous appearance on *Ring Roasts* when he tried to wrangle Scott Hall out of the ballroom after he disrupted the entire event and attacked a comedian on stage. But hey, that would be something to talk about on camera.

I made an offer through Nick that was accepted, and just like that Young Stallion Jim Powers was booked. The plan was to shoot Terri Runnels's edition of *Vince Russo's Attitude* on Friday afternoon, that would wrap around 5 o'clock and she would be whisked away to an appearance for that night. Russo could go up to his room and watch the San Francisco Giants and read the Bible while we shot *Breaking Kayfabe* with Powers, then on Saturday we would put the second *Vince Russo's Attitude* in the can.

Though I'd never worked with Powers, he reached out to us back in July of 2010 and said he loved our work. I sent him some

DVDs and he emailed me back the following:

"Sean,

First of all I would like to thank you very much for sending me the 3 DVDs. They were very entertaining as well as insightful."

I do not remember what I had shipped to him, but clearly it wasn't *Missy Hyatt's Pajama Party*. Back to the email—

"When you get a chance please call me personally so that we can discuss doing something together in the near future. Your product is the most professional and classy thing out there and I would love to be attached to that. Thank you in advance.

Sincerely,

Jim Powers"

Well as I said, that was in July of 2010 and though I didn't ring his phone, I did book him for a KC show a mere seven years after reading his email. Seven years. Aren't I great?

After booking Jim for the *Breaking Kayfabe* appearance in October 2017, Nick reached out to me a few days before the shoot. Seems there's a problem with the schedule. Jim has asked if he can shoot either earlier on Friday (Answer: No, because I have Vince and Terri coming in and we have to nail that show before Runnels is taken from my set to make an appearance somewhere else.) or Saturday (Answer: No, because we have Russo at a convention appearance Saturday morning and then as soon as Shamrock is done signing, we are shooting his editions of *Vince Russo's Attitude*).

Nick called back. Powers was upset that we weren't rearranging our schedule to accommodate him on Friday.

I'll retype that.

Jim Powers, who agreed to a slot on Friday night that *I created* when his promoter called and asked me to book him, was now angry we weren't juggling the production schedule of our new series that covers the explosive Attitude Era with its head writer and the stars of the WWE. I told Nick, rather succinctly, that we have a slot on Friday night if he wants it. If not, that's it.

I was putting the eighth coat of red exterior paint on my front door so I was already frustrated when I saw an email from Powers. It said: "Call me" and other than the fact that it was sent from his Verizon Samsung Galaxy smartphone, it offered me no other information. I put the roller down and prepared for the kind of phone call unique to producers of entertainment. The talent was about to create a problem—not the set design, not the writing, not the crew, not the flights, not the promoters, not the money, not the show…but person that should be most flattered and appreciative that we've taken a chance on them.

I paced the house, my mouth agape, as I listened to a very different Jim Powers than the one who wrote me a goddamn love letter seven years prior. He was mad that I was treating him like a "jabroni" by prioritizing Vince Russo and Terri Runnels over him.

I'll retype that.

Jim Powers, who took an open slot I had between shoots of our new series about wrestling's biggest boom period of the last twenty years, was mad because I was making him feel less important in our slate of shows that weekend. I know—you're going, "He took the gig! He agreed to the schedule!" And of course, you are right, because you are sane and therefore, not in the wrestling business.

But the stupid ass with red paint on his fingers who decided to begin producing this kind of programming ten years ago stood there on the phone and nicely explained that we were booked on this other project already, and I created a slot for him and we wrote a show that we would fit into our Friday night. I did not yell, "Jim…I need this episode of *Breaking Kayfabe* about as much as I need this fucking phone call right now so the money is off the table and so is the show!"

I did the talent relations thing and even resorted to the, "Hey, a fellow Jersey guy wouldn't insult you, brother." He laughed and it disarmed him. I assured him that Vince Russo and Terri Runnels were not seen as any more important than him. It was just scheduling. He explained that he wanted to have dinner with his daughter that Friday evening and couldn't fit the show in. I didn't want to come between a family situation, one that had apparently arisen and been agreed to after agreeing to do the show we had just written for him. But hey, family is family. What could I say?

What I did say was that I'd be willing to extend the workday of the entire crew on Saturday, now costing us more in pay as well as the expense of providing another meal for them, and shoot Jim's show when we wrapped Shamrock and Russo at around 4 p.m. It was all I could do for him. We left it there. We thanked each other, agreed to meet up the following Saturday, and I went back to wondering why in Christ's name this red paint was going on so thinly.

I did make one more phone call.

I called Kayfabe Commentaries' co-owner Anthony and explained the entire exchange, at which point he no doubt reminded himself how great a decision it was that I dealt with all talent relations. I asked him to write an edition of *Breaking Kayfabe* for Vince Russo, in addition to the Powers one. From talking with Jim, I had a feeling this booking was on shaky footing. I have a sixth sense about people and my conversation with the "new" Jim Powers, seven years removed from the email he sent me, told me he could flake out with a change in the wind's direction.

If a show falls through before production, then that carries minimal inconvenience. I'll cancel the hotel, tell crew they have the day off, and we shelve the script. We can shoot it next year, so most times the writing is not wasted energy. But when a show goes belly-up while we are on the set, that's catastrophic. So I wanted to keep another show in my pocket for that weekend. Russo was in town for the two days anyway. If Powers pulled a Powers—or a Konnan…or a Jake The Snake…or a Buff Bagwell—we would just bring Vince down and nail the *Breaking Kayfabe* with him instead. We'd be set up for that show anyway.

If you're a fan of our content, then you already know the world saw the release of *Breaking Kayfabe with Vince Russo,* and not *Breaking Kayfabe with Jim Powers.*

My Friday was plodding along fine—Vince's flight was on time and we had about an hour before Terri touched down at Newark. We were able to grab a cup of coffee and catch up. I can count the number of times I've gone to the airport myself to grab talent. I'm usually buried in production issues and Brian or Craig from our team or the booking agent himself heads to the airport. But the last time I had Vince in town it was an absolute catastrophe. You'll get that entire story later if you're not fully convinced to start any business *other* than one centered around wrestling.

So Russo was in-hand, Terri was airborne and we'd see her soon, and Jim Powers was likely looking forward to a nice dinner with his daughter. All was right with the world. I could sip my coffee and enjoy counting the "bros" Vince was dropping as the caffeine jacked him. I did ask him how Terri was, because I'd never worked with her. My discussions with her were very pleasant and she said she got a good vibe from me and she already loved Russo. She said she could talk with him for hours—always a good sign for a producer of talk show content.

"She cool?" I asked.

"Bro, total sweetheart. But bro—she's a lot."

"How do you mean? Like demanding?"

"Bro…she's a loooot." That 'loooot' hung out there for a few seconds. I just nodded and sipped my coffee. That's fine. I knew girls that were a lot. I'll listen and nod. I'll carry bags. All good.

I got the text that Terri had landed so Vince and I headed over to her baggage carousel where I met Terri, her bags, and her dog.

Terri is the tiniest little lady, but could immediately fill the biggest room in the castle with her personality, as well as dogs and bags. We headed out to my car that was prepared for people and bags, though not necessarily dogs and this cart-thing for the dog. The little guy was very cute, even tinier than Terri. I just didn't know what to do for the dog in a car. Do they get seat belted? He was the size of a cotton ball, how the fuck was that going to work? She had a pillow gimmick to lay him on, but he weighed nothing. He would have slid all over the backseat as I drove. How well trained was he? We were in my Mercedes with cream interior—shit skids all over the backseat would've been an issue.

Everything went fine. Terri sat in the backseat and held him, and he was the most well behaved living thing in the car that day. You wouldn't have even known he was there. He didn't smell, didn't bark. Well, he lived with Terri. He knew not to even try to get a word in.

For the trivia-obsessed fan, here are the KC shows that

featured dogs on our set. Does Jimmy Kimmel deal with this?

1. *Vince Russo's Attitude Starring Terri Runnels.* He sat in his cart-thing right beside Terri for the entire interview, just outside the frame of Camera A.

2. *YouShoot: Chyna.* She held the dog on her lap for the entire two-hour interview without a peep. The show sucked, but the dog was great. I should've interviewed him.

3. *Breaking Kayfabe with Marty Jannetty.* He arrived with a small entourage, so the dog probably wasn't his. But it was there.

Terri's dog was so well behaved, as they all were actually. But we were running late. Terri's flight was delayed out of Florida, so I was on the phone consulting with Anthony during the ride back about how this would work. I'd agreed to a "hard-out" for Terri at 5 o'clock so she could get to an evening appearance somewhere. We were headed out of the airport at 2:45 and it was a half-hour drive to our set. Terri said she needed to "freshen-up."

"How long will that take?" I asked her. Before she could answer, Vince tapped me from the passenger seat.

"Bro—forgetaboutit."

"Just like ten minutes," Terri said from the back seat.

"Bro—half-hour...*easy.*"

"Oh, shut up, Vince," Terri said through laughter. I felt like I was backstage at RAW watching them argue about segment times.

Regardless, our cameras probably wouldn't be rolling until 4 o'clock, and that was generous. But since promoters and their drivers are sometimes late, I decided we would power up the set, start shooting, and whenever they grabbed Terri, we would cut. I told Vince and Terri to have the same clothes available the next morning and we could get up early and nail the second half of the show. We would edit it into one seamless interview, and that's what we did. See, you never knew.

Now, lest anyone forget that by splitting Terri's show across two days we were adding a *third* shoot to our Saturday schedule—first the pick-up for Terri's show on Saturday morning, then Shamrock's edition of *Vince Russo's Attitude* in the afternoon, and a full set turnaround for the Jim Powers *Breaking Kayfabe*. Throw a couple of meals in there somewhere, as well as a convention appearance for Russo and there's the kind of day that makes me double-up on my Nexium.

After Terri was picked up from our set rather promptly (unfortunately) at 5 o'clock, we prepared to break for dinner. It seemed we had the rest of the evening free so I asked Vince if we could grab that edition of *Breaking Kayfabe* that I'd told him was tentative. Powers was still slated for Saturday, but we had some time on Friday night and Anthony and I thought we should just get it. We shot the show and wrapped. The following day was going to be a monster so I was quite happy to have loosened my tie and undone my top button, free to head home shortly after 9 p.m.

Before leaving the resort, I headed into Yogi's bar and grill to say goodnight to the crew and maybe grab a quick scotch before I hit the road. There were some things I was not surprised to see in there—like Brian Knobbs and Jerry Saggs, The Nasty Boys, at the bar. But alas, there was also something I *was* surprised to see—Jim Powers drinking at the bar.

Powers looked very comfortable; the glass that sat before him was likely not the first he'd been served to that point. Seemed that dinner with his daughter wrapped up a little earlier than he'd predicted when he told me he would not be available at all that night.

Do I go in?

No one saw me yet. I could turn and walk out, shake Jim's hand tomorrow afternoon, shoot his show, and that's it. I could pretend I didn't know I'd been worked—just pay all the expenses associated with the additional Saturday shoot, and save myself the headache. I could play along.

"How was dinner last night, Jim?"

"Great brother, great. Good to see family."

Of course, that's not what I did.

I walked to Powers and squeezed myself between Knobbs and Saggs. I introduced myself to Powers, whose eyes were nearly shut. They actually did shut intermittently during our discussion that followed. His words were very slurred as well. My guess was that he was very, very tired. Must've been there quite a while.

We had a chat that went around in circles for about fifteen minutes, with the Nasty Boys standing on either side of Jim and I at the bar, throwing in their two cents and stirring the pot.

I'd reminded Jim that I added a slot in the schedule for him. He again told me I made him feel like a jabroni because I wouldn't shoot his show before Terri's and Vince's. I'd reminded him that we agreed to this schedule, and then I changed it for him and agreed to Saturday.

Then Jim said Saturday was now no good. I should add a Sunday! *What?!*

I told him the whole thing should have been cancelled after he told me he had to go to dinner with his daughter that night. Saggs laughed and turned to Powers.

"You told him that's where you were tonight?" he said, howling. I pressed for details about the dinner and a timeline that got him to the bar well before 9 o'clock, though he couldn't shoot with me. Then Saggs pressed him too, sensing more drama could come and further annoy the shoot interview mark with the wrinkled shirt and undone tie, looking like a salesman after a Labor Day sale.

Powers said something about an airport trip he had to make. Saggs pressed him more. I was uncomfortable and just said, "Let's forget this whole thing, Jim."

"No wait," Saggs said. "You had to get your daughter from the airport?!" Jim had become confused and he was losing his grip on his own story. There some more eye closing and forehead rubbing before he threw out his hands, cutting off the discussion.

"It was a personal thing and I don't want to talk about it," he barked. Saggs turned back to the bar and smiled. Knobbs was leaning over tugging on my arm.

"Hey brother, why aren't you hiring *us?*" he asked, right in front of Jim. I didn't even respond. I was busy with Powers.

"Jim, that's fine about tonight. Let's just call it a misunderstanding. Are you now telling me you can't shoot tomorrow?"

"We should do it Sunday," he said. I told him that wasn't an option. With great exasperation he told me he'd try and move stuff around on Saturday and make the shoot. I just couldn't keep everyone working with us hanging until Jim figured out whether or not he'd be shooting with us. That wasn't going to work.

"Let's just get it another time, man." I offered him my hand. His head was down, despondent.

"Yeah, Brian is right," Saggs says as he turns back to me. "You should be offering *us* a spot on your show." For a moment, I actually consider negotiating something right there. I did always want the Nastys on *YouShoot*. They would have been hilarious. I told Saggs so.

"Next time you guys are out here let's do it," I said. But I still had the issue of the angry, sulking Powers sitting on the stool before me. I wanted the hell out. I'd had a busy day and there was another staring me in the face for Saturday. I put my hand on Jim's shoulder.

"Hey, one Jersey guy to another—we can do this again. I tried everything you asked for."

"Yeah, but you won't do Sunday," he said. I explained yet again about the cost and the fact that he'd agreed to two prior options. I wrapped up the ridiculous conversation and headed for the door.

"Hey Sean," Powers called out. Before turning, I prepared to explain why we couldn't do Sunday yet again. I turned.

"Where in Jersey?" Jim asked.

"Hudson County," I said and put up a fist. He smiled and did likewise.

I was spent. As I walked out to the parking lot I didn't want to even return to the hotel on Saturday. It felt like nothing was accomplished. I had half a show with Terri and Vince in the can, I'd been unable to land either of the Young Stallions, and apparently it would have been easier to work with the Nasty Boys than everyone else. Who knew?

You're probably holding this book because you're either a fan of pro wrestling and the programming produced by my company, Kayfabe Commentaries, or perhaps you are interested in starting a company yourself. You might be sitting with the germination of an idea you'd like to bring to the masses (or even better, a niche of select, passionate folk) and have no interest in wrestling. Welcome, both of you.

If I'm correct with either of those assumptions, then I now know who you are. And I know why you bought this book. This leaves you to wonder why the hell you'd buy this book by me. Fair question.

As an owner of Kayfabe Commentaries, I was charged daily with the task of creating entertaining, interview style, pro wrestling-oriented programming. We don't have any actual wrestling on our shows. It's all programming revolving around the sport's outrageous and glorious history and participants. In our 10+ years of life, Kayfabe Commentaries (KC, herein) has created shows with original and innovative formats in which to present such programming. Simply put, we redefined the genre, and our niche in the world.

The word "shoot," as in shoot interviews, is specific to wrestling. You'll see it popping up in the book. Pro wrestling, for so many years, was a closed society. Participants in the sport were closely knit and committed to perpetuating spellbinding illusion. The word *shoot* is an industry term meaning "real." So this segment of programming in which we operate, commonly referred to as *shoot interviews*, means the wrestlers are drawing back the curtain and speaking about once protected secrets. It was our goal to take the concept of the shoot interview and apply formatting never before attempted.

Prior to being a co-founder of KC, I was active in the arts and the business world as well. I've been a professional film and television actor and voice artist for over 20 years, having worked on some of the biggest motion pictures and TV series in that time. I also directed national TV commercials, short films, and was a director of photography on a feature film, back when people shot actual film as opposed to digital. I've written books, screenplays, TV scripts, you name it.

For 10 years, while working as an actor and director, I was also working on Wall Street in the sphere of the investment banking world. I wasn't a blockhead, er sorry, I mean banker. I worked in graphics, branding, and presentations. Basically, I was showing the blockheads how to be creative. Most couldn't. Their entire, Ivy League lives were spent in the confines of the proverbial box they so often read about thinking outside of. Someone had to take them by the hand and show them how to do that. That's what I did.

But while I was doing that, I was paying attention to their world as well. I was learning the world of big business from the inside. Deals and figures involving the biggest companies in the world passed my desk all day, every day. I worked to put them into attractive and digestible presentations and documents so the bank could go on to make zillions of dollars financing these massive deals with the Goliaths of business. Many working with me and under me in my department were focusing on only the aesthetic. They were artists as well–wholly disinterested to what lay inside the egg we were painting. But I was also paying attention to the machinations of business that sat before me.

When I wanted more in-depth explanation, the senior bankers were very helpful in taking time to explain their thinking in the work that was being presented. It helped that a Vice President may have seen me on *Law and Order* the night before and wanted to hear about how his favorite show is made. Or the lady banker was intrigued that I'd been working on *Sex & the City*, her favorite show, for the past five years. It was a quid-pro-quo I guess. They thought it was cool to hang with me and talk about Hollywood and I needed pieces of their MBA as I was starting my company.

I also spent a few years in real estate but was very quickly bored and frustrated by the rigidity of that industry. I'm an entrepreneur and control freak. I can't so easily hand over so much of my destiny to someone else. That's what real estate is.

As a real estate agent you are nothing more than the waiter—bringing stuff back and forth. Your decision-making is removed; your creativity is grounded. Within a few years in real estate I found myself in a sea of desperate goons with no business acumen, always waiting to get lucky. There were exceptions, though very few. Most of real estate is snake-oil sales and tactics. There were corner cutters and liars with holes in their shoes.

So I went into wrestling production. Hold your laughter.

Another reason I view real estate as a dead-end business is that it's almost completely market driven, and we'll discuss that danger later in this book. I have always viewed sectors that are totally controlled by the performance of a market as death traps. If the market is up, things are good. If the market is down, no one eats. There's no opportunity to create multiple revenue streams or build hedges. Actually, you can't build anything! If there is nothing to sell, and no one is getting a mortgage approved, you're screwed. Again, no control.

My experience in both the worlds of entertainment and business truly puts me at the intersection of art and commerce. I understand both. And it is my job at KC to ensure they work together cohesively. We need to create art—quality, enjoyable, profitable art.

That's the fluffy stuff. If you're more business-minded you'll probably want to hear that we'd grown revenue 695% in our first six years of life. More notable than that number was that KC did it during a recession, and in a most challenged category—digital media. Within our first ten years in business, I got to present our people with a Lucite award thanking them for their part in our surpassing $1 million in gross sales by 2015. It didn't just land on our doorstep. You'll read everything I learned about how we made that happen.

And before you hang a medal on me, know that we also got torpedoed by the digital media market. We were in a segment that didn't change and wouldn't accept change. Our fight continues to this day and you'll be right beside me to experience my analysis and game plan in the final chapter of the book.

And that right there, is exactly why you bought this book by me—successes and failures. Yeah, I know—the crazy stories, too. They're here.

There's a lot of blood in wrestling. The stars have been gouging their heads to draw a crimson mask for decades to excite fans and ramp up the drama. But there's another kind of blood of which I will be speaking.

I call KC a *Business of Blood.* That is to say, a business rooted in its owners' knowledge and passion for the niche they serve. We're fans that started a business, and that alone gives us insight and an advantage over big companies. We're a very small company and that's a good thing. I will spend the next couple hundred pages sharing with you why I think the structure and practices at KC are applicable to almost any small business and why it gives one a leg up on the big boys. If you love GI Joe dolls, have collected them for years, and are about to start a GI Joe-oriented business, my money is on you, even before Hasbro.

This book is broken into four parts:

Part One: The Business of Blood - This outlines the foundation for the entire business principle in which I strongly believe. It's what the whole book is about and, hopefully, your entire business will be about.

Part Two: Running It - In order to keep your Business of Blood afloat, making great product, and making money, you will need to tend to it constantly. I guarantee that you have no clue how much attention this will require. In this chapter we will delve into all of that.

Part Three: Growing It - If the Business of Blood is a self-sustaining operation, then you've cleared a major hurdle. Maybe you're one of the 20% of businesses that make it past the first few years alive. Well 90% of those will be gone in the next few years, so you better get good at growing your Business of Blood. This chapter covers growth and expansion, when it's possible, and when it's not. We tried some stuff that didn't work and probably worked against us. It was a great lesson in the limitations of a Business of Blood, and how success puts blinders on you.

Part Four: Saving it - The climate changes, and sometimes it never changes back. It will be your job to have your company change and adapt to new market environments. Sometimes it's related to simply trends, but other times you'll see a permanent shift in our world that affects your business. It isn't simply weathering a storm—it's global warming. If you're a media company like us then you're dealing with a lot of that as of this writing.

Throughout the book I've included real-life examples from my experiences with Kayfabe Commentaries. Each anecdote pertains to the topic we're discussing and is included to illustrate more vividly the concept I'm conveying. Wrestling fans looking for stories from the insane world of wrestling will find them here was well.

I thank you for taking the time to read this. Let me know if you found it valuable. Finally, I want to thank my partner in business and co-founder of KC, Anthony Lucignano. The results I speak of are as much his doing as mine. It is the Jagger/Richards or Tyler/Perry that teams strive for. Though Anthony always prefers to reference far geekier comparisons like Jobs/Wozniak or Lee/Kirby. Either way, the result is the same—magic was made from two people seeing the same apparition one day.

Of course, those other guys didn't try to book the Young Stallions.

Part One:
The Business of Blood

1. The Blood: It's the Passion Flowing Through Your Business

I WAS ON the phone with Lanny Poffo, a talented wrestler of years past and brother of the legendary "Macho Man" Randy Savage. I'd seen Lanny on some shoot programming produced by other companies and I thought him to be candid, intelligent, and entertaining in a real "left-field" kind of way. I'd never worked with him before but I thought he'd be great for a show called *Breaking Kayfabe,* wherein we explore the personal lives of the men and women of the sport. To say they are colorful outside the ring is an understatement.

I thought Lanny was interesting and suspected he'd be loaded with the kinds of quirks and idiosyncrasies that make for humans of a fascinating mold. I had no idea that discussion of bidets and self-fellatio were to ensue. But Anthony and I just had a hunch.

Additionally, and maybe more importantly, Lanny was the closest human being to one of the most mythic and shrouded big names of the sport, in his brother Randy. Lanny is no idiot—he knew we wanted a piece of the late Macho Man, as did most of the people who rang his phone. But we truly wanted lots of Lanny too. How many of the mouth-breathers of the 70s locker rooms could quote Chaucer and sing Rodgers & Hammerstein? Lanny was unlike the pack, and I knew he could go toe-to-toe with me as I led the dance. Shit, he could probably lead it, like so many of our great guests could, Cornette and Sullivan to name a couple.

But yes, it was Hall of Fame season and Savage was being slighted again, it seemed. The WWE would again produce their HOF show and announce a slate of entrants into the supposedly hallowed halls, and again without mentioning Macho's name. In years past they'd mentioned Koko B. Ware's name, Tony Atlas's also. Edge was in. So was Nikolai Volkoff and Sensational Sherri Martel. I couldn't ask Randy about it—he was gone. But I knew if I sharpened the pick axe and chipped away, Lanny would unearth the jewel. Whether by conjecture or gospel—Lanny could shed some light.

So I spoke with Lanny and prepared to give him the pitch and sheepishly confess that, yes, I was interested in his growing up in a wrestling family, buttressed by patriarch Angelo Poffo, wrestler and promoter, and also his brother Randy. But I was also wanted to talk about Randy and his grudges with WWE, their grudges with him, and the whole sloppy sordid affair that makes for YouTube click-bait and fascinating shoot programming.

Lanny agreed to it all, including the revelation of a few details no one had ever heard regarding Randy's aversion to ever working for WWE again, including its Hall of Fame. Lanny didn't know me. He hadn't worked for us before. Why did he entrust us with something as dear to him as Randy's legacy?

The Blood.

"I have seen your shows and I see the care and the production value," he said. "You guys are passionate and knowledgeable and if anyone should have this story, it's you." I was honored. And I agreed with him.

A business born out of its creator's passion has a distinct advantage over most big businesses. Some of those big businesses may have been started 100 years ago by one individual's passion for something. But here we are a century later and the current form of that mega-corporation may resemble little of the early form.

Passion and business are almost unrelated—might even be diametrically opposed. It's right brain versus left brain. The passion that was the genesis of an inventor's idea could easily erode over the years. It may have been deadened by going public, analyst estimates, directionless growth, expansion into unrelated market segments, and numbers overtaking an emphasis on innovation. The company went from what I call *inside-out*, to the colder *outside-in* structure. More about those later.

I despised many of the tenets of big business when it surrounded me on Wall Street. The process is cold, predictable, and repeatable. I didn't see challenges to one's creativity. I saw a rote process.

What I was actually seeing was an absence of passion—an absence of Blood.

This is why I would bet on a business run by a passionate entrepreneur, or small group of similarly passionate entrepreneurs, in a sector in which they are entrenched *as consumers and fans first.* I think that particular business has a better shot to satisfy the consumer, attract attention, and achieve longevity.

It actually goes beyond being passionate about a sector of the market. The entrepreneur must be a passionate *participant* in it. If you never bought a ticket to a wrestling show, bought a magazine, or stood online to meet "Rowdy" Roddy Piper, how can I trust you will be able to produce a product that speaks to me? There should be a real intimacy and knowledge that can only come from first being a consumer and fan of that market segment. In many cases, big businesses have lost sight of the consumer experience, which is why the business you would start tomorrow would have a leg-up on them.

There have been exceptions to that perception, of course. Apple was, at one time, a big business filled with passion. Their Blood, infused by co-founder Steve Jobs, was evident by the success and innovation of their product line. Jobs's personal beliefs in simplicity in both design and function—serving the user's desires (whether or not they knew they even desired them)—became the entire brand.

They committed to Jobs's unique vision beyond just product. Their marketing reflected that passion, producing ads that remain bold and unforgettable, even thirty years later. Go and YouTube their ad "1984" or "Here's to the Crazy Ones." I'll forfeit my man card here and admit that the latter ad has brought me to tears. It's beyond an advertisement. It is a manifesto for Jobs, his company, me, probably you if you bought this book, and so many others.

That "Crazy Ones" commercial has two versions with two different narrations—one by Jobs and one by Richard Dreyfus. Watch the Dreyfus one. It's better.

Only a company filled with passionate developers, programmers, technophiles, and artists could so successfully meet the needs of their audience. They were the underdogs at one time, dwarfed by the massive market share owned by the PC companies. Apple users were not consumers—they were fans, a gang. Today they've become the giants, but at one time they were the cool minority.

In short, Apple *was* their market. They were developing products for themselves. The folks at Apple were passionate fans of their field. Most of their employees would probably have been consumers of Apple products even if they weren't employed there. They were fans first, who got lucky enough to land jobs in a field and at a company about which they were passionate. Therefore, they'd intrinsically know the answers to questions that they would face in product development.

When deciding to launch Kayfabe Commentaries, Anthony and I had The Blood working in a dual track. Our passion was both wrestling, as fans of both the product, as well as the aftermarket offerings like newsletters and shoot interviews, and also professional production. My background in film and television, on both sides of the camera, positioned us to have an advantage in that aspect of what became our market segment.

I was a long-time pro wrestling fan, as was Anthony. He had experience in production and computer programming. There were a host of elements working for the embryonic KC there. We didn't really know any of this in 2007 when we decided to find wrestlers, bring them to a hotel room, and record Mystery Science

Theatre-style commentary tracks for wrestling matches. We were fans. We thought of a product we wanted to own. So we made it.

We had no business plan. We hadn't even incorporated. Who had time for that shit we had lightning in a bottle. We just wanted to make it.

So against all practical business advice, I got on the phone, found some guy named John Mills from Indiana who was advertised as a cat that booked talent. It was literally that fast—about an hour's worth of discussion with Anthony, assurances that he had the equipment to record and sell these downloads, and I was dialing Mills after finding his name on the late Georgianne Makropolis's website. It was probably better that I had no formal business training, because all that would have gone right out the window the moment I ventured into wrestling production.

The Blood as my guide, I cut a sideways deal with John Mills for the services of both The Honky Tonk Man and Greg "The Hammer" Valentine. I say sideways deal because in essence, by going through Mills and the talent directly, I bypassed the promoter that was bringing them out to my area to work some shows. Did I know protocol exactly? No. But did I know someone else was footing a bill for airplane tickets, hotel rooms, and food while they were out here? Of course. You can read all the details in my book *Kayfabe,* wherein I outline the entire escapade.

We went through elaborate plans to avoid that promoter and get our product. That promoter footing the bill was Super Agent Eric Simms, and I wish I'd avoided him better. Jesus, he actually just texted me as I write this. I'm not put him over and telling him that he was making his way into yet another of my books. He'll become more unbearable.

In truth, he became indispensable to our company and we ended up working with Eric for years and years afterwards.

But back in January 2007 while getting ready to buy some gear and make rock and roll in the garage, we didn't know all the things that are so important in building a sustainable business, like branding, marketing, customer service, or any of that shit. But we had The Blood, man. I knew if I sat down in front of a microphone and chopped it up with these guys, we'd have a product that fans as passionate as me and Anthony would love. If we loved it, fans would probably love it too. It would be just like them sitting there conducting the interview. We all shared The Blood.

Also in that Blood was my fastidiousness for production. We would be mic'ed well for our initial mp3 products, and lit, shot, and produced well for our videos, which would come soon after our launch.

So wouldn't you prefer to buy your pro wrestling programming from a company passionate about both the sport and the elements of production? I thought a company like that would have a good shot at making greatly entertaining programming. And I think we delivered from the get-go. Within a year of our having launched our *Guest Booker, YouShoot,* and *My Side of the Story* series, people in the business were coming up to me asking "Where did you guys come from?"

So as a passionate entrepreneur, you're ahead of most big businesses already, in the category that matters most—your product. How's that for a shot of confidence up front?

Some of the talent we worked with early on could see what was to come. Before we had any inkling of just how influential we'd become, I heard JJ Dillon on an Internet radio show discussing his forthcoming appearance on our show *Guest Booker.* He saw the innovation in the concepts we had in the hopper—we hadn't even released our second series *YouShoot* yet. But we mentioned the concept to him, as well as *My Side of the Story.* On that radio show, JJ said we had some groundbreaking things coming for the wrestling aftermarket. We didn't put him up to that.

The Honky Tonk Man was another guy that could feel the winds would soon blow at our back. He was our first guest on our now-signature series *YouShoot,* and shortly after we shot that episode, we ran into him again at a hotel bar in Carteret, NJ. We were killing time while waiting for Greg Gagne's delayed flight to land in Newark and Honky arrived at the hotel. The bar was filled with fans, other shoot companies, and wrestlers. When Honky came in, he bypassed the room and pulled up at our table.

"You know you guys are gonna have the best thing out there," he lead off with. I don't even think he said hello. It was like he'd been thinking about telling us this. "You got the fans participating in this and asking us all the questions. That's gonna be where it's at."

He saw it. Where's The Blood? It's with the fans, obviously.

2. Know Your Market, Part I: Know it Like a Fan

I'D MISSED BILL APTER'S call. The venerable editor of pro wrestling's finest magazines back in the day had left me a message saying he had an idea he wanted to run by me. I love Bill. Not only is he wrestling's most prized journalist, he's a great performer and a true entertainer. Bill was our Roastmaster for our *Ring Roasts* series so anything he had to pitch me, I was ready to listen to.

About a year prior to this phone call, Bill pitched me a show that would have been fun to attend, but one we could never record or sell. Bill has a fondness for karaoke, as anyone who attended the taping of *YouShoot LIVE: Dixie Carter* can tell you. Our guest of honor was late getting to the venue so I asked Bill to entertain the crowd and within ten minutes, the sport's most respected authority was standing on chairs singing Sinatra and doing duets with KC wack packer, The Hess Express.

So a year prior to the missed call, Bill pitched me a live show wherein wrestlers did karaoke. That was an easy rejection—we couldn't sell the songs that were being performed. We didn't have the rights. Might be a fun night out for Bill and some of the boys, but it wasn't a show for us. But Bill had a year to cook up something new so I was anxious to get back to him and find out.

"Hey Sean," he began, "I have an idea for a live show that we can shoot on the Friday night before a convention so all the wrestlers in town can participate."

"Okay, like we did for the roasts and the *YouShoot: LIVE,*" I said.

"Right. We can get the bar at Yogi's in the Crowne Plaza and set up a stage. I'll have the wrestlers come in for the show and we can do karaoke with them."

I thought someone hit rewind on the tape deck playing out my life.

I re-explained the licensing issues and how that wasn't something KC could sell. But more than that, as a fan, I'd be amused for about ten minutes of watching Fred Ottman do "That's Life," or perhaps a haunting rendition of "Turn, Turn, Turn" performed by Smith Hart. After those ten minutes though, I'd be questioning why I spent $20 on this show. It wouldn't sit well beside copies of *YouShoot* or *Guest Booker* on the DVD shelf.

Just like those passionate Apple employees, you have to know your market from the place of a passionate fan. That's The Blood.

When you know a market so intimately, there are no big surprises. You're so much more prepared to deal with the myriad of issues, obstacles, and wonderful challenges posed by working on products that you love as a fan. You'll know your market like you know a loved one. (You'll also need to know it like a scientist, but that's coming later, thus the Part I here.)

Intimate, enhanced market knowledge has many benefits. It goes beyond cold data, and I'd argue that it can't be learned without a passionate, personal investment.

Let's take an example of a fisherman. Fishing is in his blood. He's been fishing since he was a little boy—his first trip to the lake having been 25 years ago with his father. They would fish for hours and his father would help pass the time by regaling the young boy with tales from his own boyhood fishing trips with his father. By osmosis, there is much more than a mechanical learning that is taking place. The boy is ensconced in a culture of fishing. The sagely advice and associative instincts are being infused into his very soul.

The aforementioned mechanical learning is also very important. As the boy grows, the feel of the rod, the amount of bait, the seasonal advantages to fishing in certain months, the feel of a bite—all of this information is being seeded and reinforced over and over again. It becomes etched in the subconscious. Let your child bang on the piano keys if they show an interest in it. Something is happening there.

As this fisherman grows from boy to adult, he's invariably had successes and also mistakes from which he's learned. He's honed his craft. He sees it as so much more than a hobby, due to all of the mechanical and cultural reinforcement. It is part of his life, both his conscious and subconscious. It is The Blood.

When this fisherman takes an entrepreneurial plunge and opens a fishing supply store, will he not be at a huge advantage? Of course, we're all nodding our heads. We didn't even have to pause and think about that one.

But why were we so instinctively certain as we answered?

It is because we trust The Blood, and we all do so very much by intuition. We can quickly spot a car salesman that doesn't love cars. He'll likely not make a sale to us. Your customers will also identify you and your company's Blood.

If we open our scope a bit we realize the extent to which this fisherman knows his market. We tend not to think of our passions in a business framework, but do so for a moment and let it take us as far as we can conceive. Consider how many aspects of the market this fisherman has touched and acquired an enhanced knowledge of. We'll hit the obvious ones right away—he likely knows everything there is to know about fishing rods and which bait and lures work well with certain types of fish. But let's go deeper. He'll have enhanced market knowledge of:

- Boats well suited for certain waterways
- The weight of effective fishing line, in specific scenarios
- Locations that offer good fishing opportunities
- Great resorts near those destinations
- Filleting and preparing types of fish
- Effective sunscreens
- Techniques for spotting fish activity
- Sonar and other electronic aides for big fishing

That's a wealth of knowledge beyond simply fishing. It is enhanced market knowledge, extremely personal and intimate. This fisherman could likely offer his expertise to so many varied segments of that market. He's versed in equipment, boats, technique, travel, clothing, electronics, and probably much more as they relate to fishing. There are a host of businesses that can be launched from that knowledge base. If he entered the marketplace, I'd put my money on that guy. He already has a massive competitive advantage due to all he intrinsically knows about this market. He already knows what his customer base wants because it's *him*.

His competitors and their businesses had better have The Blood, because this guy is gonna be moving fast. He'll be developing products he knows his customers will buy. His more formally business-educated competitors will be wasting time and money on market research to mitigate risk. Naturally, that's what their MBA classes have told them to do. But while they're asking fishermen what they want, our fisherman is already in development with a product fishermen need.

3. Passion vs. Business Acumen

THE FISHERMAN EXAMPLE is a very stripped-down illustration. There's a big piece of the puzzle that is of great importance and its absence can sink this fisherman fast. (All pun, baby.) He may know the fishing market and The Blood will arm him with the greatest advantage for his business' survival, but if he mismanages the business it will eventually fail, or at least operate with greatly compromised success. He will still have an advantage with customers. But over time, the structure could crumble around him if he doesn't learn the basics of business.

We've all hired contractors for some service. Some are better craftsmen than others. Some are better businesspeople than others. That's the law of averages. As a consumer, which are we more tolerant of—a good craftsman with poor business skills, or a poor craftsman with good business skills?

I'd venture to say we've all tolerated the first of those choices, but have eliminated the second from our lives very quickly. Our glistening, perfectly installed hardwood floors will mitigate the fact that the craftsman was late to our house, doesn't advertise effectively, and can't balance his books. Devouring a restaurant's succulent *Pasta alla Norma* prepared with authentic Sicilian flair will likely outweigh the fact that it took a long time to hit our table. Same for the fact that the restaurant's menus aren't in the Yellow Pages, and the restaurateur isn't being very economical with his vendor choices.

Conversely, if the hardwood floors were stained unevenly and scratched, how much would it matter that he was on time, has high market visibility from his nice billboard ads, and manages revenue well? If the pasta tasted awful, would we care that it was served quickly in a restaurant that markets and manages properly? You get a bit of a break if you have The Blood and can deliver it to your impassioned customers.

Both The Blood and the business are important. Without The Blood, that craftsman would be at a disadvantage in his workmanship. He would not have been able to advise us on what type of wood and stain would be most economical, durable, and beautiful for us. Physical workmanship is always an indication of passion too. The chef would not have been able to replicate the Sicilian origins of the pasta so accurately had he not been passionate enough to travel and experiment at length for his craft.

It is this advantage that resonates with consumers so greatly. It keeps you in the game even if there's an absence of the business skills at first, and if you are adept enough to realize you're lacking them, you have time to fix it. The glistening hardwood floors and delicious pasta buy you lots of time with the public in the form of repeat business and flowing revenue while you work on maximizing your business.

A wonderful product born out of The Blood is irreplaceable and of the utmost value to the lifespan of your business. It's the sustenance that touches the kindred souls of your audience and keeps them coming back. They know your passion first-hand and they appreciate it.

Business skills are learned. They deal in cold numbers and the interpretation of them. If you're astute at it, that skill will be of prodigious value to you. But it's an assumable practice. Give me some time and I'll tell you what this data or that data means. But The Blood can never be learned or taught. It is for this reason that The Blood usurps business acumen as a prerequisite for starting a Business of Blood.

The Blood resonates with your customers and creates that all-important kinship between them and your company, and also with you, as its founder and owner. That kinship is what causes companies to explode in popularity via social media and viral messages. Social media presence is so vital and the entire advertising business has been redefined by it.

It's so comical when I see cold businesses trying to capitalize on a passion that doesn't exist. Bottom up marketing (more later) is a more organic fit for some businesses than others, but some insist on trying to "wear" it. It stinks when we smell it and it rings so unauthentic. It really resembles an 85 year-old man walking into a club dressed like 50-Cent.

Don't you laugh when you pick up a package of sausage that has a label saying, "Follow us on Facebook?" Well-educated businesspeople know about social networks, blogs, and the concept of personalizing their products, but they fail to realize that simply applying the buzzwords doesn't get it done. It's not just clothing you throw on your business. There is no doorway to cool. You got it or you don't. And if that sausage company is going to make me follow their social page, they'd better find a very compelling reason for me to do so. What can you do with sausage on Instagram? Sounds like a question on *YouShoot*.

Within the first year of KC's existence, we launched that series, wherein all the interviews are entirely conducted by fans' questions. There was no master plan in giving a series over to the fans and I supposed it was far ahead of its time back in 2007. But something in us caused us to go social with the series.

There's a risk in that, of course. Relinquishing total control over the content of your product to fans could anchor you to their limitations. You might end up asking the size of Batista's dick to every guest on your show. Trust me.

We did retain a little control of *YouShoot*. Anthony selects the questions that work best for the show and the guest. Then while I'm sitting there with cameras rolling, I'm scrolling through the shooting script to grab the best questions, and the ones that we haven't touched on yet. Did we ever take out a little more insurance than that?

Yeah. We have.

I should probably begin by saying that we get hundreds and hundreds of questions for every edition of *YouShoot* via email, video, Twitter, and Facebook. And 99% of the questions asked on the show are from those fans. And sometimes, friends, we must help the show along. Is this a betrayal? Is it a little like saying, "Honey, I've been 99% faithful to you?"

But truthfully I don't think it's a betrayal at all to throw in a question here or there with the goal of getting the best possible product for the viewer. If there is a story that fans didn't know about or just didn't ask about, and we know the guest will be entertaining or provocative in their telling it, then we have to add it. Time for Noel Medina or The Assassin from Jersey City to fire up their fictional laptop and plant a question. Oh, stop being all offended. Wrestling itself is a work, you know.

It's all about touching the fan's soul with your content, and if planting the occasional question makes that happen then so be it. I live in service of the fans.

Customers will become members of your congregation when they sense their Blood is mixed with yours, your company's, and your product's. The sausage company has a marketing department that has identified, very coolly, that Facebook, Instagram, and Twitter are hot trends and businesses are becoming a part of it. Then know that viral trends are honest and valued so much more than top-down techniques of yesteryear. But they've clearly made little effort to examine why Facebook and Twitter find symbiosis with certain companies.

If your Business of Blood is to be built correctly, it should be built around your passion and your product. The centerpiece is The Blood and the framework is the business. Too often you'll see people trying to "start a business." There are magazines and bookstores filled with advice on how to spot market needs and just whip up a business that serves it—finding the market first, then manufacturing Blood.

Man, that's a counter-intuitive thought process. It's not wrong, per se. It doesn't mean that businesses started in such a cold fashion will fail. Actually, chances are if they have strong business acumen and they can hire people with a passion for that industry, they'll succeed. But that isn't what we're talking about here. That's all science. They're lost in a business plan and the color of the logo—focusing on cold stuff. They're lost in the business. If there was a true passion at work in that entrepreneur, then those items would seem like tedious distractions on the to-do list.

Forget that shit, let me get busy building this thing, man.

That should be the attitude. You're being taken away from building this amazing product to try and articulate that passion into some cold business plan software. Ugh.

A herd of educated suits trying to find excitement about a product or business that's entirely functional and cold is a dirty job. Someone does, indeed, have to do it. The sausage company needs a person to wake up every day and get excited about being its marketing director. I have no doubt there is a way to do it, but I cannot imagine how they do.

4. Bad Blood

THE BLOOD ENSURES a remarkable competitive advantage as you build your Business of Blood, but there are occasions when this can be your downfall if not identified and managed properly. Many of the decisions you'll be making with your heart will be good ones, fortified by the love of the subject matter in which you're dealing.

But how many people do stupid things for love? A lot.

Your scientific knowledge of your Business of Blood will, at some point, come into direct conflict with your heart. This is where you will make mistakes, I guarantee that. Passionate folk like you and I tend to listen to our hearts.

It starts with the germ of an idea. This idea bubbles to the surface from that wonderful place inside us where there lives a fan of our own work, and of the market in which we operate. It sounds something like, "Wouldn't it be cool if…" or, "You know what would be awesome…" And you best believe that idea would indeed be cool. You know this because The Blood has ensured that you're a fan first—a participant in the industry which you now serve. You have the instinct of which we've spoken so generously.

That impetus, the "wouldn't it be cool," is likely what founded your business in the first place. You spotted the gap in your market because you were already a fan and a participant in that space, and you wanted something more. Fortunately for you, many other people decided they too wanted something more that you now provide. And they're grateful.

But here comes another "wouldn't it be cool" idea, sparked in the shower or on the ride to work. Naturally, you welcome it with open arms. Such curious intuition was the birth of your company and its product line, so now it seems like a gift about to be given again.

Be cautious. Your new potential enhancement to an existing product/service/program/store or whatever you built is born of the best intentions, however your system of checks and balances now needs to kick in and temper the excitement. By the grace of God, you haven't gone broke yet unlike the 80% of small businesses we hear about all time. Here you stand—successful and well served by the intuitive power of The Blood.

Well, not entirely. You started your business because of The Blood. But you're still in business because you are now becoming (or you were to start with) savvy in business as it relates to your market. You were able to get to the next level and tame the wild horses inherent in Businesses of Blood's early days. Discipline and an adherence to a set of personal rules have kept you profitable and growing. And that's exactly what you need to keep this latest *"Eureka!"* moment in check. For a few minutes, we're not going to be a fan.

The move of a successful business from innovative startup with an abundance of The Blood, to sustainable operation requires the discipline and long-term perspective often lacking in the entrepreneurs that founded the company in the first place. Most often, the founders are eventually moved aside after all the pieces are in place and skilled managers come in and scale the business properly and work on business development. There's a tangible "Phase II" that occurs simply because the ingenious founders are the wild horses and they may ruin the operation as it grows beyond their wildest dreams.

A great example of this is ESPN, the cable sports channel that is now an institution. The story of the network's journey from radical start-up (What? A 24-hour sports station airing small-time college football games and something called Australian rules football?!) to established standard bearer is brilliantly charted in Anthony F. Smith's book *ESPN the Company* (Wiley, 2009). In a Cliff's Notes-type encapsulation of the fine work, Smith categorizes the all-important move of the company from the hands of the visionaries and founders in the "Start-Up" stage—in ESPN's case it was Bill Rasmussen, Stuart Even, and Chet Simmons—over to more seasoned businesspeople in the stage Smith defines as "Survival."

In a most succinct illustration of the needs and requirements of said stages, Smith uses the allegory of the *Pioneers and the Settlers.* It's an easy connection for all to make—can you imagine if the rebellious, wayward drifters that discovered the land actually tried to run it? After the finding of—or taking of—the land, folks must come in who can form a government, settle disputes, and form communities.

Thank you, Mr. Columbus. Kindly step aside now.

This process isn't foolproof. After the leadership transition, there exists the challenge of trying to retain the spirit and value system of the visionary founder(s). There are countless examples where visionary companies have lost their way after the founder leaves or is removed. The story of Starbucks is a great example. Howard Schultz built the coffee empire, left, and was compelled to return to serve as CEO in 2008 when financial constraints and questionable business decisions muddied the brand, and damaged the company. Those who succeeded Schultz after his initial departure failed to keep the visionary's code that founded the company. In this case, losing the wild horse almost lost the business.

Okay, enough history. There you have two opposing examples on each end of the philosophical spectrum when it comes to moving from the founding stage to the management stage. In ESPN, who moved the founders aside, we see a massive success story. The company has become a defining sports entity and is now a property of Disney/ABC. In Starbucks, after Schultz was gone the heart of the initial brand was lost in the rapid expansion of product lines. Schultz was able to come back in and restore order, making Starbucks the monolithic monster in coffee.

What does that tell you? It tells me that each case is as individual as the people we're talking about. There's no doubt that initially an innovative business needs a visionary disruptor at the helm. Beyond that phase, it will only last if it is run with disciplined management and focus.

We should all strive to be innovative and disruptive visionaries with great discipline and management skills. Maybe we can be both Phase I and Phase II in our business's life cycle.

And that brings us back to our Business of Blood. Now we must reign in our latest *"Eureka!"* moment that has come to the surface. Our very cool, new idea needs to be viewed with our "Phase II" eyes. Man, I hate the "Phase I" and "Phase II" shit. It reeks of blockhead business-speak. But there is a point to be made in identifying the different mindsets.

Your new idea has to move your business forward and not harm it in the long run, and your initial excitement can cloud your judgment. This new idea is a great one. It will introduce a new element to your already innovative and trendy core product/service. It's a real game changer, says you.

The first hurdle you must give yourself to hop is asking the question: *Why hasn't this been done already?*

Seems simple, but man, is it important. Don't skip this step. Why aren't your competitors, who need cash flow just as much as you do, already doing this? The question may have an obvious answer, one that you can find just by knowing the competitors in your market. You probably patronized them before you started your company. But more than likely you're going to have to dig for the answer. Is your idea really *so* innovative that no human being in this market has thought of it? If it is, then you have your answer. But it probably isn't. Maybe there's a horror story out there as to why this new product line or augmentation to an existing product is not happening elsewhere. Maybe it's illegal. Find out.

If you have an answer and you are still proceeding with your idea, then it's time to set up your next hurdle. You need to put your idea up on the lift and do a diagnostic on it. You're so excited you might rush into this without checking for the following signs of preventable trouble:

1. Cost of this new idea is too high in relation to expected returns
2. The new idea will either hurt or stray from your brand

Both of these would be Bad Blood—passion that may satisfy the fan in you, but also hurt the company you founded.

A year or so after we started KC, I was watching the U.S. presidential debates during the election year of 2008. Before us stood arguably the two most powerful men in the world, exchanging their ideas and philosophies for the public. I had a powerful image, one that would work well for our outside-the-box programming that we were beginning to develop. The Blood showed me a program that only we would dare produce—a presidential style debate between two of the more powerful and influential men in wrestling's history.

Bruno Sammartino and Harley Race were two wrestlers of the 60s, 70s, and 80s that were world champions in their respective, rival federations. Bruno was WWWF's anchor for a couple of decades and drove business to such a height for the McMahon family, that their federation was able to keep a cash cow milking the Northeast until the younger McMahon was able to go national via the cable TV model. Simply put, if you lived anywhere between Maryland and Maine and watched WWWF, Bruno *was* wrestling.

The NWA was a massive network of smaller wrestling federations spanning the entire U.S. outside the Northeast. Harley Race was a legit badass and held the NWA world title 8 times, ruling all of those wrestling territories that fell under that NWA umbrella. All combined, those bundled territories made the NWA the largest and most powerful wrestling conglomerate ever. And Harley was a guy that carried the massive undertaking of representing all of those territories here and all over the world.

See where I was going?

Bruno and Harley had long since retired, but they were never put on-camera in the same room to go through their careers and the business in general. And with the U.S. presidential debates pounding our televisions, we had the perfect format. Harley and Bruno, each standing at their own podium, fielding questions about wrestling's history and future direction, could have a presidential-style debate. It would be produced under our "Investigative Specials" banner, and could be a powerful addition to the wrestling historian's library.

I was on the phone trying to make it happen. I was excited. The Blood told me what an entertaining program this would be. I spoke to the respective booking agents, put all the figures on paper, and then Anthony and I were armed with the info we'd need to greenlight it.

But the cost was steep. We were booking this through a third party and there's always a little risk in that when you aren't talking to the talent directly. Is the agent or promoter giving them the proper details about your show? The "shoot interview" has come to have a dirty connotation in the business and I always thought what we did transcended that label. But it was what it was—we were a shoot company.

Let me pause the business lesson with Bruno and Harley and say that Super Agent Eric Simms is notorious for this. He admits that he tells his clients "as little as possible" about their bookings.

He proudly proclaims this and it's part of his strategy, I guess. But when we receive his talent and they're clueless or annoyed as Simms is on his way out the door counting his money, it's frustrating to say the least. He's reliable and hard working, but his quirks are a nuisance.

After famously dropping a bomb on our *Ring Roasts* show by attacking a comedian, Scott Hall was finally booked to be on *YouShoot*. It was an Eric Simms booking and the price was right. Eric had done his job by packing Scott so full of bookings for his stay out here, that the prices had gone down significantly. It was an easy negotiation with Eric. I think we went back and forth twice, and Eric managed to meet my price.

Once we got situated on the set and I sat down beside Scott and prepared to jump into the show, he started bellyaching about the money. It's always a joy to launch into those discussions when we're under the lights, wearing microphones, with a slate board in front of our faces ready to clap and start the show. Great for establishing on-camera rapport.

"Well this is the deal Eric negotiated for you," I said. See, I always go to logic during confrontation, idiot that I am.

Eric Simms, of course, was nowhere near the set, tending to other clients at some other booking. But there we sat, ready to roll, and Scott serves me up a heaping dish of this shit. If he were on the set of some TV show or film, would he wait until the slate was in frame before looking over to the director and complaining about his fee? Would this not have been handled well in advance? Part of my job in dealing with talent is to shelve the insult and deal with the problem at hand, which was money. And sushi.

"I'm just sayin," Scott began, "the envelope is a little light, and I got people coming to the lobby to take me for sushi."

"You want sushi?" I asked. "I'll get you sushi. We can eat it on camera, throughout the show." A pathetic attempt at humor to diffuse the situation.

"The money is just kind of insulting. I want to see these people and they're taking me out for sushi, so we better just get going with this." This was Eric's bundling of Hall's commitments and ill preparing him for us. An agent should have been aghast that one of his clients would insult an employer. That's in the real world. In wrestling, no one gives a fuck about anything.

In *Kayfabe* I talked about the first few minutes before a cold shoot, wherein we have no time to become acquainted with a guest, as being indicative of what's to come. Scott was ballbusting and pissing me the hell off. Once you commit to a price you just go with it and take it up with your agent later. That's my thinking. In Scott Hall's case, I should have told him that his offer would have been higher but I deducted damages from *Ring Roasts* five years prior.

Instead, we just rolled the cameras and like so many in wrestling, Scott Hall delivered a hilarious and honest edition of *YouShoot,* answering everything asked of him and dishing the dirt when prompted. So many of yesteryear's performers are gifted with that performer's gene, always able to rise to the occasion. I will deal with the dickiness of a talent as long as the product is great. It makes it hard to host and appear jovial and chummy on camera, but you do it. It's about the show.

Getting back to our faux pas with the presidential style debate back in 2008, Harley came back as a confirmation, but I was told Bruno's offer was too low. It was a tough spot because without both men, the show was obviously impossible. It wasn't an easy decision. Our initial offer on money had been countered considerably higher by the promoter. Would we go that high?

Anthony and I hemmed and hawed a bit. I was haunted by the recurring phrase "for history's sake." And when Anthony put the ultimate decision in my hands, that phrase caused me to make a mistake. I greenlit the show. I listened to only The Blood.

Make no mistake, for history's sake this was a great decision. To this day it remains the only time both champions appear on-camera together talking about the sport they dominated. But from a fiscal standpoint, I didn't step out of The Blood and see that the market for the wrestling historian offers a smaller share of sales. When we can design programming that touches a few markets at once, finding the historian but also the younger fans, or just fans of revealing, edgy stuff, those shows do the best. Back then especially, when we were in the process of redefining this shoot programming market, this was singularly geared toward the old-school wrestling historian. And simply put, those shows don't sell as well. Kevin Nash outsells Bruno Sammartino. Jim Cornette outsells Harley Race. The shoot market may be the only place where that happens, but it does.

It's all relative though. You don't stop producing programming geared to the wrestling historian. But you have to budget those shows accordingly. Either that or you have to simultaneously hit another, more salable element. Our shows with Cornette, the loudmouth, outspoken wrestling manager and booker, sell tremendously because Jim is a true student of wrestling history but also wildly salacious and vitriolic. The historians eat it up, as do the younger fans who want the uncensored venom Jim directs at those he despises in the business. He's also wildly entertaining to listen to. His gift of gab and phraseology is unparalleled on camera.

But Harley and Bruno's show, titled *The Great Debate '08,* would be straight history and perhaps a bit dry as well. I should have known better than to overspend on something I probably suspected would have a marginal return. Did I even know it would have a marginal return at that point? I don't know. We were in the shoot game just over a year and likely didn't have enough supporting data. The Blood made my decision. It showed me pictures of how the historical significance of the show would drive unexpected sales. I based this on nothing more than hope, and The Blood's false promise that others would love it because I would. Sometimes you have to be much more honest with your gut.

The show was entertaining, but it was predictably dry. We simply weren't yet at a level where we could command enough attention in that marketplace to propel sales to the levels we needed for a show like that. A few years later it might have been a different story. But back in 2008 we were still wild horses—revolutionizing our industry and trying crazy, innovative things to carve our niche. We should have employed a little more discipline.

This is an example of preventable illness #1 listed above—*Cost of this idea is too high in relation to expected returns.* This one is simple to avoid, as it just requires honesty, market knowledge, and a pencil. As years went on I didn't ever consider a large scale, costly venture without a realistic pro forma—a speculative financial breakdown of expected costs and returns. I actually do multiple pro formas, using a set of variables for each one—best case scenarios, worst case scenarios, higher costs, lower costs, etc. In the end, you need to know how much you have to sell in order to get the return you want.

If you do this accurately and honestly, you'll be able to better judge whether or not new ideas are good ideas for business. If it shows up as a bad idea on paper, you might not want to discard it just yet. Work a little harder to find a way to make it work. Maybe there's a hidden revenue stream you didn't consider that would tip the scales for you a bit. Maybe pay-per-view, T-shirts, a live audience, and a meet and greet would have delivered enough to justify doing *The Great Debate '08*. Probably not, given the costs of those.

At Kayfabe Commentaries, our live events always ran a tight pro forma. We didn't do many. We shoot almost all of our programming in controlled, studio-style setups. However there were some occasions where we ran live tapings, with an audience, and sizable expenses. We co-produced the *Ring Roasts* series of live, celebrity, comedy roasts for pro wrestlers, as well as a live version of our popular, uncensored series *YouShoot*. Margins were slim and extremely variable. They depended on long-range results with the eventual release of the DVD, in exchange for lots of up-front costs. It was a tough model, a risky one.

The addition of iPPV, which is streaming Internet pay-per-view offered to fans around the world, changed the model in our favor. Now the immediate offset to the expenses wasn't limited to only the fans in the building, nor did you have to wait six months for the DVD release to deliver that revenue. Our ticket sales were now truly global, as fans driving to the event in Jersey could see it at the very same time as a guy in Belgium, via his computer. That additional revenue stream tipped the pro forma for us.

The second form of preventable illness you might encounter when considering a new decision involves a much larger scale issue and can harm your company over time, and much more severely than a one-time expense error. When you betray your brand, you're in trouble. In many ways, it's everything you are.

5. Brand

ONE OF THE ancillary duties of Kayfabe Commentaries is to sometimes secure other bookings for the talent we are using while they are in town. Many times they already have multiple bookings, KC just being one of their stops, and we all bump into each other at various events over a few days. Terry Funk asked me when he was going home every time he saw me for an entire weekend, and we weren't even the ones who brought him out.

On one of those multiple-event weekends, we had a vendor table at a Pro Wrestling Syndicate show. They were a very professional indie company that ran a great show, booked great talent, and drew great houses for an independent. We'd had a great business relationship with their company until their flea-bag booker tried to fuck me on a deal, shortly after he split with the company and its very capable owner Pat Buck, under similar circumstances. More on that sideways deal later.

On this night we partnered with Shane Douglas on a vendor space at the recreation center packed with fans. Earlier in the day between shoots, I overheard that the promotion really wanted Shane Douglas to be a part of their card that night, as they were doing a tribute to Mick Foley. Shane trained with Mick when they first started out, so naturally it made sense to have Shane up there to honor Mick. There wasn't going to be any significant money in the shot for him, but I wanted Buck to have him. Shane was at the same resort as we were that day doing a convention, and though he wasn't a guest of KC's that weekend, I like him a lot and I offered him a spot at our vendor table and a split of the merchandise he brought to our table. He took the gig and was appreciative.

Also at our table that night was the venerable Kevin Sullivan. Kevin was always one of my favorite guys to hang with. He's full of wisdom and listens as intently as he talks—a rarity for a wrestler.

This was Kevin's first time at a PWS show and I'd been telling him about their great crowds and he sat there at our table and marveled at the fed's operation. The action was great and the fans came in droves. The federation used established talent, mixed with wrestling students from their school in New York. On that night, one of the trainees did an "ass spot" in a match which, for all of you readers of Margaret Atwood out there, is a part of the match where a wrestler's trunks are momentarily drawn down in the back, exposing his backside and causing him great embarrassment.

Problem was this trainee didn't pull the damn trunks back up. He may have thought it was funny and if it was just a quick flash you could pass it off as a comical accident. But this frigging kid wrestled for about five minutes with his ass out in front of 800 people. I knew it wasn't a good thing—there were cops and building officials there. But Sullivan started going crazy.

"No, no!" he was yelling from our table as he watched what was going on in the ring. He had no actual stake in the show; he just knew a problem when he saw it. "He's gonna lose this house! Text your friend and tell him to send word to that kid to cut that shit out!" I pulled out my phone and texted Pat. "Oh my God!" Sullivan went on and didn't stop for the whole time the cheeks were out under the hot lights, adding quite the fragrance for the ringside fans, no doubt.

Eventually the kid pulled himself together and finished the match with his tights up. As I understood it, Pat went nuts on him in the dressing room when he returned. And I knew why, as did Kevin Sullivan.

The kid was damaging the federation's brand.

Comedy spots are okay here and there, even for a roughneck company like PWS. But the fact that this kid worked almost and entire match with his brown eye winking at the audience went beyond what that company should have been doing. It wasn't hardcore and it had ceased to be funny. It was stupid even after just a minute or so, and that was not what this federation was positioning itself as, with regular appearances from ECW legends and other tough guys like Fit Finlay and Mick Foley. This kid standing in that ring later on that night apologizing to the crowd so Pat didn't lose that house was softening that brand. It sucked. I felt bad Pat Buck had to be a den father. But I got it. His brand was at risk.

Brand is one of the most overused and least fully understood concepts in business. As a consumer we're usually dealing with brand in the most incorrect way—as a label, rather than an identity.

"We need dish detergent, dear."

"What brand?"

"Cascade."

As a business owner, that should trouble you. If your brand is nothing but a label, you're on your way toward the depersonalization and the oblivion of cluttered shelves. The label isn't the brand.

There is also sometimes unjust emphasis on just the visual elements being one's brand. Your logo isn't your brand. Your colors aren't your brand. They should be *indicative* of your brand, carrying its message. They should evoke the qualities on which your brand is predicated. But these elements just adorn your brand, not unlike one's sport coat might tell us something about their personality.

Your company is very similar to a person, and you should probably think of it like one. There should be traits and characteristics consistent with its brand. This is your company's personality, simply put. And the most successfully branded companies have such strong personality, we know immediately when we are watching an advertisement for them. There exists a flavor that's carefully crafted and associated with that company.

Apple is a fine example. I know what to expect from an Apple advertisement. I know the tone of voice, I know the attitude, I know it will be cool and perhaps a little irreverent. Their logo is a friggin' white Apple. Does that logo immediately speak to the company's personality? I'd suggest it's everything *else* about Apple, from their sleek innovative products, to their smart and inspiring advertising, that reinforces the brand. More so than the little Apple with a bite taken out of it.

Branding is very important. Large corporations have an entire department dedicated to maintaining the integrity of its brand. Again, a lot of emphasis is placed on the physical, and though it may be your company's calling card, it is secondary to some more important features. The physical aspect of your brand should only be reflective of the internal elements of that brand. Those internal elements are what you should labor over, worry about, and fight to protect for the long-term. You can change your logo as much as you want, I guess. If you have to compromise something, let it be the physical element of brand. In rank, your brand is comprised of:

1. Your promise
2. Your product
3. Your design

Promise

First and foremost, your consumer needs to know what to expect from you, and they will only know that if your promise is clear. Promises will vary from industry to industry, but it's what all commercials should be selling to us. Ads for home security systems always show some man in some uniform, vaguely law enforcement, and a room of stone-faced officials monitoring charts and gizmos we assume to be watching our home when we are gone. The visuals alone promise us safety and the swift hand of justice at our side.

What do car companies spend their time promising us? Many

times we see the shiny vehicle taking turns on empty, country roads. I directed an ad just like that and we spent a great deal of time making the car look sexy and fun. There's the promise for those ads—fun. Sometimes though, we see slow motion, crash test dummy shots in a car ad. Safety is the promise being made there. Next time you see a car ad, ask yourself what the promise is.

Product

The next most important element to the overall perception of your company's personality is your product. Apple can position themselves in the minds of consumers as uber-cool innovators only because their product line is seen as very cool and innovative. The product has to deliver on the promise. Seems basic. If Apple's product line were just clunky and unattractive knockoffs of already existing electronics, it doesn't matter how much emphasis they put into the commercials, print ads, and store layout. The product wouldn't keep the promise that the advertising makes. The consumers would see it as bullshit.

Have we ever strayed at KC? Of course. We're content providers so there's naturally a tendency to produce a variety of material. The real trick is keeping it similar enough, while different. How's that for a frigging task? Innovate, but don't change.

There have been a few times when we went too far out into left field. I love countdowns, so here are the **Top 5 Deviations from KC's Brand.**

#5 - *Bombshells* - On its surface, talking about pro wrestling with the ladies of the sport is not much of a deviation at all. But we didn't really probe the inner workings of the business. The modern era of wrestling doesn't make for good, protracted discussion. Nothing in wrestling today, whether male or female, is behind the curtain—the magic is performed with the audience seeing all the strings. That series was a heartfelt attempt at paying tribute to the ladies of the ring, but the indie stories failed to regale fans and even the fans of today's ladies federations didn't want to hear much chatter.

#4 - *Next Evolution* - See above, add penises.

#3 - *The Great Debate '08* - Bruno Sammartino and Harley Race sitting down and talking the championship eras of WWWF and NWA is certainly a concept that is consistent with KC's brand. But we wrapped it in this stupid, mock debate setting to play off the U.S. presidential debates that year. It made for a clumsy format and because I served as moderator only, unable to interview them and ask follow up questions, the show sank as I watched.

The entire reason I appeared on-camera as the host of KC's shows was so I could ensure the result. I usually guided the conversation, pressed when I needed to, and asked poignant follow-up questions. In this show, I did none of that. It was a softcore debate and I had two of the most legendary champions in the same room! And I did nothing with it. It was a failure of epic proportion—I took two world-class chefs and asked them to make sandwiches. Fuck me.

#2 - *Ring Roasts* - ...because the celebrity comedy roast is the natural home of the retired wrestler. Trying it with The Iron Sheik made sense, since he was doing the comedy circuit with comedian Bob Levy and some *Howard Stern Show* cast-offs. But I'm not sure it should have been us doing it, and I now know for sure it should have stopped after Sheiky.

#1 - *Missy Hyatt's Pajama Party* - It was such a deviation that I actually enjoyed the challenge of figuring out how to do it. If you were the commissioner of the NFL and you were forced to stage a ballet to open the Super Bowl, that challenge might be fun. But good Lord, it doesn't belong there.

KC was becoming quite well known and we were lauded for our innovations and risk-taking. That false sense of security sometimes allows you to make the mistake of thinking people will respect *any* attempt you make to do something different. And to me, that's what we were doing—producing something different. Couldn't we take the stars of the ring and create programming that spotlit their talents and didn't necessarily follow a shoot interview format? I thought we could.

I still thought we could when we produced *Raven's Restler Rescue,* which I still think was great. That show was much closer to the heart of what we do at KC, as it drew the curtain back on the business and let fans see the creation of a wrestler's entire gimmick. It didn't succeed, but *RRR* was not a deviation from brand, so it wouldn't belong on this list. It was just a new flavor of coffee.

But the pajama party thing was the result of an overdose on the success of our company and the cult-like dedication of our fans. We screwed them a bit there.

For the record I think Missy did a good job hosting. It wasn't easy—the concept was very broad. Anthony and Missy prepared the format and created the questions. We had a large white board off camera so I could communicate with her during the show without breaking the spontaneity of the girls frolicking on the bed.

Oh yeah…for those that didn't see it, I suppose there should be a brief synopsis:

Missy Hyatt, Lacey Von Erich, and Amy Lee sit on a giant, silky bed for an hour and a half, play games, grab boobs, make prank phone calls to wrestlers…tonight, following the Nightly News!

I thought it went exactly as we designed it to. It was funny, provocative, and for the horn-dogs we had a "Fake an Orgasm" game, as well as the "Real or Fake" touching segment. Fun for the whole family. And for the record, on that very same set just three hours later, Jim Cornette shot his genre-defining edition of *Guest Booker.* When we told him what he'd missed he asked if I sterilized the room. And me and Jim's on-camera relationship was born.

Your product will help define the personality. You may need to tweak the image you're creating to be more consistent with what you're selling, or vice versa—rework your product. But you need to have them both in alignment. If you want to own the place in the consumers mind as "safest" then the place to start is with your product if it isn't really the safest gizmo of its kind. If you're looking to own the "coolest" space, ask yourself—is it really the coolest? Actually, screw what *you* think. Ask a 12-year-old.

If your answer is "no" to any of the branding questions specific to your market, then you need to get back to work on the product. You probably just need to tweak. You've created a Business of Blood so you're not like one of these serial entrepreneurs, grasping at products to justify owning a business as opposed to the other way around. You're building your business to justify your product born of The Blood, so the product came first and therefore was likely mostly intact. But you may need to make small adjustments. Maybe you have a dynamite product but can't find its personality or don't know where to position it in the existing marketplace. You need some help finding out because it's very important. For some extensive study, Al Ries and Jack Trout are masters of branding and I would start with their book *Positioning: The Battle for Your Mind.* After that, you should work your way right through their whole collection of insightful books on this topic. But I do understand how busy you are, running your BOB. Check out just a couple of them.

Design

Now, after your promise and your product are aligned with your vision, you can examine design. Does the design fit that image? From the logo, to your colors, to packaging, to the visual elements in your advertising—you must send the same message. Colors, font type, taglines…there are plenty of things to consider in design. There are great books and online resources available about the physical branding of your company. There are psychological elements to color, shape, texture, and even the name of your product or company. Kayfabe Commentaries is a long name, a bit confusing too. It's a long URL also. I wish we'd taken more time to consider this years ago. There had to have been a better option out there, though I don't know what it is. I'm too used to Kayfabe Commentaries and anything else sounds wrong. But I know I hate giving my email address to people over the phone. Learn from my error.

As of this writing, a popular trend in naming businesses seems to be snappy words that have little to no relevance to the product. Seems everyone is designing a name to fit comfortably on an app—Airbnb, Uber, Zillow, Venmo. Out of context, these words do not immediately connect the consumer's mind to a particular product. But it's the trend, so Grug may just be the right name for your line of sunglasses.

Once the promise, product, and design are congruent with the personality you are trying to project, you can say you've truly established your brand. Now the hard part—maintaining it. Remember, you're not going to have an entire department dedicated to managing the company's brand like a big Fortune 500 company. I've seen it first hand in my time around big finance. If a firm's logo is light blue and someone wants to prepare an advertisement in which the logo is dark blue, or any other shade, the branding department is involved, probably panicking, and meetings are being held. Companies are that staunchly protective of it.

The physical branding should be the least of the violations you'll safeguard against. Your product decisions will do more to reinforce or weaken your branding. It's a very nebulous thing, but it's important to monitor. All your product decisions need to be weighed against both financial implications, and also brand. It's easy to decide to crank out a product line that will make money. But if that product line in some way violates the ethics or the pattern that your company has spent time building, its brand, then that's a shortsighted decision that should be reworked. Would you forfeit long-term success for a quick hit? Think in the long-term. It's trading $100 every week for a lifetime, for one payment of $500 today and a gamble on tomorrow.

It happens all the time. Most CEOs don't consciously do it. Many executives just do not realize the long-term, deleterious effects of muddying a brand. But because there is no immediate price tag attached to it, it doesn't register on their radars as a cost. Companies that end up diluting the strength of their brand always do so by chasing quick money. They will add a hot, new, product line that is completely inconsistent with their brand. Adding sandwiches to the menu at the cool coffee beanery will make some lunchtime sales but you just cost yourself points in your efforts to become the number one coffeehouse in the consumers' mind when someone suggests grabbing a cup of Joe.

In my not so fictional example here, those sandwiches replaced the telltale aroma of carefully crafted cups of coffee brewing, with the smell of melted cheese on a grill. See the stupidity? Eventually they did too and Starbucks eventually built a system of heating sandwiches in machines that emitted no residual odor. Might sound silly to you, but it was one of Howard Schultz's major directives in returning to the company.

If done tactfully, a company can add a product extension without damaging brand. But it's a very individual, case-by-case consideration. Each company needs to consider its own product lines and make their own decisions. Coca-Cola did not so severely damage their brand by creating Diet Coke did they? Or caffeine free Diet Coke? How about Coke with Lime? Probably not.

But how about adding a line of Coca-Cola doughnuts? It's still food isn't it? Who wouldn't love a tasty doughnut, washed down with a cold glass of Coke? Just like the coffeehouse—who wouldn't love a tuna melt with your large latte? Do you see the disconnect? You should. Coca-Cola would never step on their brand like that. Nor should the coffee company have done so. It's all about long-term positioning in the mind of the consumer.

At KC, we are a production house and content provider, with several series-based shows in production. We have a unique branding situation that we share with movie studios and TV networks—there is an overall company brand that must be maintained, but also a bunch of small brands for each of our series. Each program has an identity and a personality that must be considered.

When people bitched and pissed and moaned about new programming—*"my God…why Russo, or Cornette, or Nash, or Sullivan, or Dixie?"*—I invoked the TV network example, asking if FOX was allowed to produce both NFL programming as well as The Simpsons? One show is for these people over here, one show is for those people over there, and some people will like both.

What was harder for me to understand was that we were stepping on a viewer's personal brand when they objected to programming. I often use the rock band analogy when talking about what we do, and not just because it makes me feel like I'm cool. Our fans are not the dispassionate fans of the FOX network. Those viewers would watch The Simpsons or the NFL regardless of what channel they were on. How many of you guys give a second thought to what network is airing the show you like?

With us it's a different ballgame, and fair or not, we are judged on a different scale. So many of our viewers are fans of ours and entrust us with their Blood—the handling of their passion. They take great offense when they feel we've mishandled it. Intellectually they may know we have to produce a little something for everyone. But their hearts want what they want, and they kinda want us to cater to their every personal desire.

We've strived to touch a couple of markets with our programming—historical, nostalgic, and on the other end of the spectrum we touch a more unpredictable, irreverent, comic-based market. For the historian we have our series *Timeline* and its subsequent spinoffs, as well as the newer series, *Supercard*. There's our series *Guest Booker* for those interested in the creative aspect of the wrestling business, with a touch of wrestling history thrown in. Our investigative specials probe very specific, individual aspects of wrestling history. And we also have some lighthearted, freewheeling programming like our series *Wrestling's Most* that is, in essence, a countdown show of fun topics. We also have the very edgy series called *YouShoot* that is not for the faint of heart, but always a lot of fun. It's a fan favorite.

Each of these series is unique in its branding from the standpoint that each episode of a particular series should look alike, sound alike, be lit similarly, and deliver the consistent promise of that series. But each of these series should differ from one another. *Timelines* can't look like *YouShoots,* and so on. The company's brand is different from the series brand, and each series brand must be different from each other's. Confusing? It's really not. For the branding of shows, think of the TV network example and all of the different shows that appear on that network during the week. Here's a comedy, here's a news magazine show, here's a police drama, and here's a football game.

So what is our company brand? In keeping with the example above, what is that network's brand? What is the thoroughfare of all of our programming that ties them all together under our banner?

Our programs are united by their production values being the top in our segment of the industry. People expect a KC show to be flawlessly mic'ed, lit, shot, and edited. They expect some post-production graphics to enhance the experience. First and foremost, there is an audio/visual expectation to KC shows.

Our shows are also always uniquely formatted and seek to take the viewer inside the business from an angle never before explored. Is that our brand? Partially, yes.

Remember, brand is more than a singular tagline, despite what some may errantly say. I also consider our rapid, first-class customer service to be part of our brand. Our accessibility to our fans and the invitation for open dialogue with them is also unique component to our company brand. I also realize I am a part of that company brand as frontman. Our viewers are used to seeing me on camera drawing information and secrets out of my guests. In one year we dropped three new series with hosts other than me, and they're all referenced in the cancellation countdown a few pages back. I'm not saying that's the reason they didn't take off, but from what I've read online and in my inbox I know it didn't help.

We offer a lot of emotional ownership to our viewers. Conceptually, our shoot-style programming is innovative and has quite involuntarily been a template for the other shoot-style programmers, the major wrestling federations, and podcasters all over the place.

6. Hire Yourself: Working While You're Working

THERE'S A DIFFERENCE between going to a job and having a business to run. This book is made for that very marketing director of Fictional Sausage, Inc, provided he or she also has an intense passion for fishing, or quilting, or gaming, or writing, or pro wrestling. Their countless hours spent finding ways to make sausage ads go viral probably gave birth to an idea or two of their own. They may be ready to start a fire and turn that passion into a business.

His or her Business of Blood will be started and operated very much outside of their Monday through Friday sausage world, probably on evenings and weekends. The Business of Blood starts as an ancillary pursuit. Kiss your free time goodbye, but you won't mind it a bit. You'll be earning a living at your shoot job, (Dutch Mantell first uttered that term to me and I love it) and pouring your passion and energy into building your Business of Blood.

Use the lessons you've learned in your job to help build your business. Is your boss an asshole? Don't emulate their behavior if you have others working for or with you. Or, maybe you'll start to understand some of their frustrations from the other side of the aisle. Did you identify something wrong with a business model at your day job? Look for those errors in *your* business. It's really more of a life lesson than a business lesson—learn. Learn all the time. Use your day job as a training ground for your Business of Blood.

Use the hours in which you're stacking boxes at your job to study which packing materials hold up well. Write that box company's name and number down. Use the hours in which you're using online business applications for your shoot job to consider which of those programs your Business of Blood will need, or what code you'll need to build your website. You'll get a sneak peek into real-world business situations that will preview what works and what doesn't. Make everything research, provided it's nothing proprietary or protected by the company you work for. You can't steal what's legally protected. But other than that restriction, you should look around. Remember, this is the cold part and it can be learned.

Talk to your bosses. Ask questions. You don't have to mention your business pursuit, as long as it doesn't violate any parameters of your job. It's none of anyone's business. Chances are your bosses will love talking about their initiatives and brilliant ideas. If they're in middle management, they'll enjoy complaining to you. Either way, listen to the decision makers at the top as well as their pawns, the people directly above you. There's value in both their bravado and misery.

Learn, learn, learn. Do your reconnaissance. Your day job is paying you to go to school.

7. Outside-In vs. Inside-Out

THE WORLD IS populated by lots of businesses that try to manufacture passion. They're functional, they work, and they're necessary. I need soap and toothpaste too. But they're cold, and very much not what we do.

Cold businesses breed a science of sameness, of process. As mentioned earlier, much of what business-for-the-sake-of-business companies do is repeatable and can be sustained by repetition of best practices. "Best practices" is just fancy MBA-speak for a company's effective procedures. In some cases the business is so cold that you can plug in another product of choice and run the business the same way, from a general procedural standpoint.

Because of this sameness and repeatability, cold businesses allow for what I call CEO-hopping. Initially, it would seem strange that a CEO from one industry could leave their company, jump over to a new industry and assume a CEO spot at a company there. But if you think about the best practices, system-based thinking, it can happen easily, and it does. The rather rote relationship between numbers on financial statements and balance sheets renders the product's identity almost inconsequential. Whether we're talking coffee beans or carpeting, the relationships between the numbers is all the same. We're just talking about growing in Jamaica instead of weaving in Indonesia. Plug in the product, and we still need our margins to be this or that, regardless of what we're talking about. It's still supply chains, manufacturing, and retail.

Nowhere is this more evident than in a business that services multiple industries. Let's look at investment banking, for instance. Within each big firm, you have different industry groups that serve different sectors of the business world. It is possible for an analyst straight out of college to start in the Energy sector, work there for two years, pitching and doing deals with gas and electric providers all over the world. Then perhaps that banker will be promoted to associate in the Aerospace and Defense sector. Before ending their career they may work in several different sectors. The numbers are what he needs to know.

This analytical process of business management is what I call an *outside-in* business management model. The company is structured in such a fashion that its management is assumable. Real estate is another good example of this. The same model for buying and selling homes is applied in every city in every state. Laws may vary from state to state so you must abide by the specific state's real estate commission guidelines. But within that state, I guarantee you each brokerage house is training their agents en masse, in the same fashion. It's turnkey.

Once again, there's nothing wrong with that. It's a model that must serve certain businesses. But it's important to identify the traits of the cold business and the outside-in management.

Outside-in management style companies confirm their assumable nature in that their operations can be taught according to a model. It's paint-by-numbers at a higher scale. In an outside-in business, you will be given market information in the form of data. You study it, learn it, and ultimately take a required action upon the data giving you the indicator to do so. Home purchasing is tanking in town, so says the data. Required action is to reduce prices on your listed homes for sale. Hopefully that will move the inventory. It's stimulus-response, data-action. If you are a hard worker and somewhat bright you can do fine in an environment like that.

If you're entrepreneurial, passionate, and wildly creative you'll be bored to death.

Businesses of Blood are managed with an *inside-out* model. The kinship between customer and company demands that the thought process between the two be aligned. The customers should feel you've read their minds and hearts. At KC's height, we were producing 16-18 original, full-length titles per year. They must all be conceived, developed, written, shot, edited, and distributed across several platforms to our die-hard but demanding fans' desires. We were exercising that muscle constantly and it led to that synchronicity.

Our decisions about projects and broader scale issues such as company direction are generated by the inside-out model. We are our market. We don't generally need much external data to tell us what we need to do. It's better to use external vision to mine ideas.

The best example of this was our launching the *YouShoot* series. If you read my first book *Kayfabe,* then the next few paragraphs will be very familiar to you. But they are the perfect example of the inside-out guidance capitalizing on an idea born out of an external source—another presidential debate no less, but with a much better result than the Bruno/Harley show. The story is worth repeating here.

YouShoot was also a great example of how taking a well-managed risk for your fans can pay off. The show is an interview conducted entirely by the public via Internet videos and email submissions. It was born in the fall of 2007 as the United States was gearing up for a presidential election, and Anthony and I were both watching the same thing, several states away.

We had recently begun our foray into DVD production with our series *Guest Booker.* I was on vacation with my family when the all the major TV stations aired the most cutting edge presidential Q&A to date—people asked the candidates questions via YouTube videos. With *Guest Booker* and its future very much on my mind, I remember sitting up in the bed thinking this could be a great segment for that series. We would have people send in booking scenarios and our guest would do a booking exercise with those fan ideas.

Down in New Jersey, Anthony was watching the same thing and thinking in terms of using this format also. When we finally talked about it a few days later, Anthony's concept was a little more risky—center an entire show around fan submitted questions. We don't do traditional shoot interviews so this would have to be all or nothing. The whole show would be done this way. That was the hook. The *YouShoot* name came to me right there on the spot as we discussed it.

The risk was obvious. What if the fan questions sucked? What if we got no submissions at all? We have the show booked and now what? We've announced it, told people they'd get to shoot on our first guest The Honky Tonk Man, or ask him anything in the world and he'd be bound to answer it.

We decided to take that risk because we are our market. Just sitting and talking for ten minutes about the questions that he could be asked convinced us to go ahead and develop the show. The people who would be submitting videos and emails were like us, complete with the same likes and dislikes about the market, we had hoped. If we were marking out over the potential hilarity of this show, then they would likely be excited too.

The marketing angle had so many advantages. The product was the public itself, literally. People would love to see themselves, as a collective group, interacting with the stars of the business. We also knew we would have to choose the most provocative and outspoken stars of pro wrestling to be the guests, and a dangerous but popular formula was built.

During a radio review of one of our *Guest Booker* shows, reviewer Derek Burgan was telling *Figure 4 Weekly* editor and radio show host Bryan Alvarez about the new *YouShoot* concept he had heard about. In trying to digest the concept, Alvarez said, "So the entire two-hour DVD is people asking The Honky Tonk Man questions and him just yelling at them and calling them names?"

"Yup," Burgan said

"That's awesome." Alvarez's reply was confirmation. It was

one of those concepts that seemed innovative but very basic to me. I had to do the innovator's test and ask myself that all-important question—why has no one done this before? I didn't have an answer but I also couldn't see any impediment in our trying.

I did drop that little revelation earlier that we sometimes slip a little something into *YouShoots* here or there to keep things moving, and we certainly had a deck of that ammunition ready for Show One. There was a real possibility that people would be so unfamiliar with the concept that no one would submit anything. Or maybe they'd be too timid with Honky. So we had a video or two made by a plant or two, along with some text questions written by our own hand if we needed them.

Did we? Yes. We needed some.

But I can happily say that the overwhelming majority of what you saw on *YouShoot: The Honky Tonk Man* was fan generated. Hey, shit man, we're fans too. We should count! But honestly, we didn't have to resort to working the show that much. After the series dropped, it exploded. Everyone knew what to do when we announced a new *YouShoot* guest, and we never needed to stack the deck for lack of content. Anything we did in subsequent shows was to add polish.

The marketing advantage in having a fan-centric show was really an afterthought though. What really sold the concept was further solidifying the bond between our fans and our company. We were becoming one.

Inspiration can certainly come from external sources. Look around for inspiration. Our access to eclectic media of all forms is like a massive learning tree bearing fruits of all kinds. It's up to us to sift through them and use the right ones as ingredients in our

Business of Blood. They can be ingredients in our products or in our operations. Outside-in may be a great management system to find best practices or run data, but the inside-out model is the one you want for the life of your Business of Blood.

Part Two:
Running It

8. Building a Moat

THIS MAY SURPRISE you, but there are shoot interview fans working in WWE, TNA, and all over the wrestling marketplace. Oh, they may not admit to such transgressions publicly. Street urchins we are, aspiring only to someday walk among the masses of the mainstream content producers. But if you're a fan of our shows then you know we've been influencing content in the major federations for years. It may have never been as egregious as we've seen since the launch of WWE Network and podcasts, but the signs have always been there.

People doing grunt-work in Titan Tower, WWE's headquarters in Connecticut, and in production, have my cell number, and me theirs. I've gotten the occasional text when they see something in which I might be…erm…interested. I might get a text after a pitch meeting at Titan Tower wherein exact concepts of ours were pitched to decision makers that have never seen a shoot interview.

"Great idea, son!"

I might have gotten a text or two, maybe even a photo, of a DVD case for *YouShoot: Jim Cornette* on someone's desk over there. Might have even gotten a text from someone who was standing in the same vicinity of a couple of WWE producers who were discussing our series *Back to the Territories* when it first launched. Fortunately they were putting it over.

Internet trolls like to flame me for past claims of our content being emulated by other companies, but the events above are true and there's simply no denying it. I'm not crying in my beer—I know Apple didn't invent the mp3 player, and I know that no one knows or cares that, depending on your source, it may have been SaeHan or Advanced Multimedia Products. No one cares, myself included, that theirs was superior to the iPod when it first came out. I'm well aware of the rules of the jungle—it's all about scale. Apple could bring it to mass market, regardless of a step down in quality or not. And I know WWE can bring *YouShoot, Ring Roasts, Guest Booker,* or an animated show ala *Wrestling's Most* to mass market, and position it as if it were their own. And it's because of their *moat*—in their case, their size and market share. Same with Apple.

If you or I created a cola soft drink company, could we realistically make a run at Coca-Cola's business? If we started a computer company could we encroach on Apple's place in the collective consciousness? Likely not. But maybe our cola is much better tasting than Coca-Cola. And our computers are faster than a MacBook.

Wouldn't matter. And the reason it wouldn't matter is *moat.* Just like a fabled castle, any successful company has a moat built around it. It is, in simplest terms, a barrier to entry.

Business is a war, or sorts. If your want your company to exist in a given industry, you have to introduce new consumers to that industry and/or take market share from a competitor through brute force. More often than not you'll be competing for market share with the other warriors in your industry. I suppose you could introduce some new consumers to your chosen industry, but realistically how often can that happen? In our fictional foray into the soda pop market, to how many people can we really expect to introduce cola for the first time? Probably none on this planet. Maybe we'll start creating billboard space on Mars. It's free right now. (As we laugh, Coca-Cola is planning this right now I bet.)

So if our hypothetical and incredibly delicious soda is to succeed, we have no choice but to take drinkers of Pepsi (we picked on Coke enough) away from their soft drink of choice. And since both Pepsi and Coca-Cola know this, they have built a formidable moat around their respective products.

When I asked if we'd be able to make a run at disrupting the business of Coca-Cola, you probably chuckled or at least recognized the absurdity of the question. Do you know why you laughed? Perhaps not consciously, but certainly instinctively, you reacted to Coca-Cola's moat, and that's exactly how they designed it to work.

What a commentary on that company's moat. The mere thought of entering their market made you laugh at the impossibility, and you haven't even tasted my drink yet.

Every company has a moat unique to their own identity. Coca-

Cola's moat happens to be its market share and thus, its ubiquitous presence. Coca-Cola has been reported to spend more than $2.5 billion on advertising in a given year. They spend that money for reasons very different from, say, a grill company, a spray-on hair product, or affordable car insurance. Coca-Cola's ads are not stimulus-response driven. There's no desperate call to action.

"Hey, that's a cool product! I can cover my bald spot with that spray. Quick, get me a pen so I can write this number down and order it!"

"I can save how much on my car insurance every year? Pause the DVR. Get me a pen!"

These are the desired reactions to such a product's advertisement. But after watching Coca-Cola's Super Bowl commercial, no one says, "I'll be back before the second-half starts. I wanna run to the store and grab a Coke after watching those cool, talking polar bears."

Coca-Cola knows that you already know what Coke tastes like. You either like it or you don't. The CGI polar bears drinking it aren't going to make you salivate and rush to 7-Eleven. Their commercials don't generally announce any changes or updates to the product. (Not anymore, anyway. Was I the only one that actually thought New Coke tasted good?) So that ad money is spent on a commercial that asks nothing of you. Coca-Cola is implanting their product into every brain watching that commercial. It's reinforcement of the brand's existence in the world. It's further digging that massive moat that made you laugh when even considering anyone attacking their market share.

Small fries like you and me have to find our moat. It's not going to be market share or size, so we have to look in The Blood for that gift. If you're reinventing an existing market segment, The Blood itself might be your moat. Your market might be so tired and played out that people will see your passion and, in turn theirs, in your work. That might get you a head start, but it might not necessarily be a barrier to entry against competitors who take your lead and emulate it. Your innovation will soon be pilfered by the copycats and then friends, it's game on. You don't own your ideas.

9. Innovation

I MENTIONED APPLE before. For a long time it was one of my favorite companies for many reasons. Not the least of which was the fact that we edit all of our programs on Mac editing software. I found their product line superb for a long time and I've been known to gush about them.

What I'd like to spotlight here about Apple is The Blood they once exhibited. Their entire product line was born out of intense passion. Their marketing dripped with that passion. Beyond just that passion, Apple and Kayfabe Commentaries shared something in common—our moat, which happened to be innovation.

How would one make a grab at Apple's market share? For a long time their research and product development was so far ahead of everyone else in the tech industry. They stayed ahead by introducing their next innovation just as their competitors began to copy Apple's previous line. They're consistently ahead of the pack.

Great companies strive to be innovators, not inventors. As we've seen, the innovator company is rarely the creator of the product they bring to the masses and are most notably lauded for. Our niche marketplace has allowed us positioning as innovators in the field of pro wrestling shoot-style programming. With much stagnation and a dearth of any variation on shoot programming, we elevated the industry. But as with any innovators, imitators are next to follow. So our challenge was staying ahead of the game, and we always did. Eventually, KC's real challenge would come with a surge in cheaply produced podcasts that flooded the streets like crack, making our high-purity coke seem like an unreasonable luxury.

For a long time, though, the video competition was always kept at arm's length. I think our outside-the-box programming always pushed us ahead and served as our moat in this market. We were always aware when someone came breathing at our backs, and we were sure to be onto what we thought could be the next thing.

By the time copycat products arrive in significant numbers in any marketplace, the innovator needs to be on to that next thing. Apple's command of the marketplace with mp3 players was being challenged (perhaps not significantly) by other manufacturers of similar music players, as well as cell phones with mp3 capabilities. Though, by the time this proliferation became noticeable, the iPhone was introduced to great fanfare and more importantly, served to further construct a moat around Apple. And as smartphone manufacturers got on the touchscreen-appcrazy bandwagon, the release of the iPad reminded all owners of those non-Apple products, just who the leader was. And if anyone forgot too quickly, they got an Apple Watch in their face to remind them.

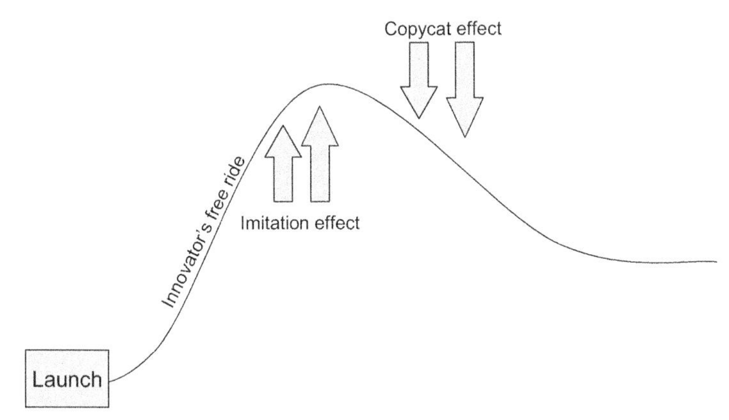

Copyright Kayfabe Commentaries

In the figure above, we see an illustration of what I believe to be the lifecycle of innovation. This was part of a presentation I made at a company quarterly meeting. After a launch, you're given a period of time where you accumulate attention and recognition. The industry is not producing what you are—either they haven't yet thought of it, or are incapable of it. This is your "free ride." Sales are all yours, positive reviews citing your innovation are all yours, and the industry watches from the sidelines. These sideliners are there partially due to an inability and/or lateness to act, but also to await confirmation. Once the waters are shown to be safe, meaning your product is a success, they'll hop in. And the waters are shown as safe 3/4 of the way up the free ride.

The first indication that the innovations were indeed successful is the arrival of the imitators. In Kayfabe Commentaries' case it was first seen when TNA aired members of our *YouShoot* "wack pack," and their Rocky Balboa life-size cutout from our show on their TV. Soon after, WWE emulated our *Timeline: History of WWE* concept and format in their magazine. There were far more obvious instances to come, but they were the first to show us the impact we were having. This, amid all the wrestling media proclamations of KC being innovators, was the confirmation that the rest of our industry segment awaited. It is at this point, the apex of our arc in the illustration above, that imitation becomes a negative, and gives way to a proliferation of copycats.

The latter upswing of the arc, after the "free ride," is actually helped along by the imitators. Knee-jerk conventional wisdom would view this proliferation of imitation as a negative, but it actually isn't yet. It is confirmation of one's innovation and also subtly indicates to your diehard fans, that you were on the ground floor of the movement.

But there is a critical mass to the imitation efforts. The proliferation becomes so widespread and the quality of the knockoffs vary so much that it is possible for some consumers to lose sight of how it all got there. Who successfully marketed the first compact disc? Who cares? But they'd better have been onto the "next thing" as I bought my first one.

The copycat effect depresses the line of innovation recognition. It will probably never reduce to the zero point, but it will most likely ride out at its suppression level.

Which is why the copycat stage should be your launch point for the "next thing."

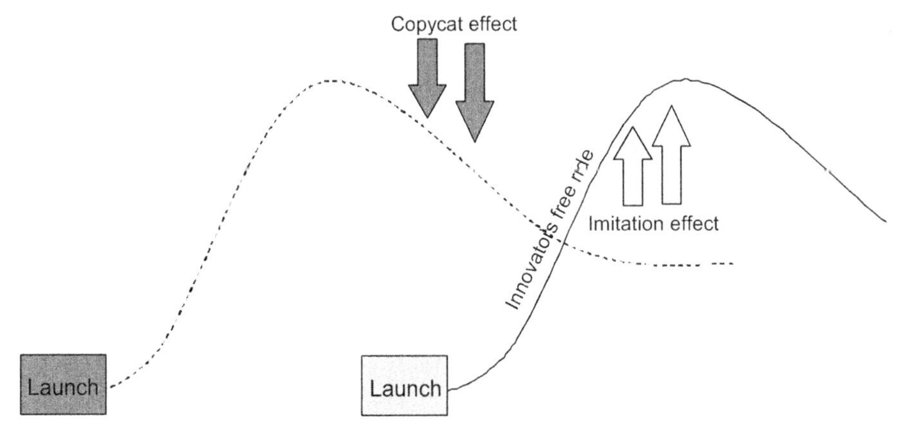

Copyright Kayfabe Commentaries

The innovation line's decline as copycats pile on will be mitigated by your next free ride. You will consistently be ahead of the market, making decisions as the rest of your industry segment considers reaction only, imitation only, yesterday only.

A quick innovation diagnostic you can perform on your company comes from a little anecdote I read somewhere. I don't remember who wrote the article but it told of the old-time war tactic where a battalion would fire their muskets, advance a step, load, and then fire again. Advance, load, fire. As they neared their target, the opposing soldiers would have to bunker down and only return fire when they could, never initiating an exchange, as the battalion continued to advance. If that advancement continued unabated, that would be the end of the bunkered group, forced to only return fire occasionally, with the advancing battalion eventually being upon them.

Which is your company? Are they the advancing battalion or the bunkered prey? Are you firing all the first shots, or are you responding to what the leader is doing? In other words, are your actions and initiatives a response to *another* company's actions and initiatives? If so, you're bunkered and they're advancing. You have to get out of that position.

The article was insightful, and gave a quick, one-question assessment as to where you stand in your market. I wish I could remember where I read it.

The story surrounding our *Timeline: The History of WWE* series is illustrative of the innovator-copycat relationship. The series is a year-by-year history lesson about the world's largest pro wrestling organization, WWE. In each episode we tackled one year with a star from the federation as they recounted all the significant events from those twelve months. The series featured a timeline graphic with callouts indicating a date and event of note, at which time the star then went into detail about said event.

The series was truly groundbreaking and since its inception, podcasts and TV shows have had stars recount specific events in wrestling history. Having the actual star there to take you through the day-to-day decisions adds an element to the show that historians just can't capture. It's as close to time travel as you'll get.

But the guests need quite a good memory, particularly the ones we ask to go back thirty years to recount their mindsets at certain times during the course of the year being profiled. We do comprehensive research and Anthony's shooting scripts for a *Timeline* can run up to 80 or 90 pages. He includes as much background detail about an event as we can fit, just in case it's necessary to jog my memory, or the memory of the guest. When possible we like to get advance scripts to the talent so they can read it and jog their own memory. Sometimes that plan works better than others.

I was beyond excited to have Bret Hart, former WWE world champion and the major star of the company for several years in the 1990s, come on and cover the year 1992. I was dealing with

Bret's agent Kirk, as well as Bret's assistant Rafaela. The show was a series of ups and downs with headaches unique to owning a production company.

We booked Bret's shoot for February 2014 at the Courtyard by Marriott at Newark. I sent the particulars to Kirk the agent, namely the money and a shooting script. It's obviously preferred that the talent flip through it and prepare in advance. Sometimes there are time constraints, but we sent the script well in advance.

We'd gotten a large breakout room and had the event catered, as we wanted Bret *absolutely* as comfortable as possible. Most times a standard suite is sufficient for our shoots. We toss the furniture into an adjacent room in the suite and build the set in the living room area. But for this one, I wanted a lot of space and decent food, so the hotel restaurant handled the catering. The room was large so we were able to designate a fair amount of space to a few dining tables with linens—a proper setup.

Bret was a film geek like me and he'd been on sets of all sizes and comfort levels. It is a high priority for me that our guests are comfortable and happy when we roll. So we got Bret's meal preferences, right down to the red wine. That afternoon, we loaded in and I checked with the hotel staff immediately to ensure the promptness of the dinner delivery for Bret, his assistant, and our crew. The breakout room was set up and we were met by Rafaela who had some troubling but manageable news—Bret's flight was delayed. No big deal really. It happens in this business all the time. I can count on one hand the number of times that my mental timeline of load-in, flight, pickup, meal, shoot, wrap, and load-out goes according to my estimation. My wife can count them too.

The reason for the delayed flight was fog. It dragged on and on, eventually approaching the time he was slated to land. He was on the phone with Rafaela from the airport so I had Rafaela tell him to ask the airline people if there were other flights that could get him into Philly or Delaware, away from the fog of North Jersey. We could go get him down there and drive him up to us. This show was too important.

Well, the shit was everywhere I guess because they were delayed into Philly and everywhere near us. The clock kept laughing at me and Bret checked in with Rafaela every half hour or so. 7:30 p.m., 8:00 p.m., 8:30 p.m. Oh, good—here's the fucking feast being wheeled in by the hotel staff.

Then Bret called again. They cancelled the flights. That was it. I was sitting in a $650 breakout room with $300 in food and drink, plus crew. Good thing they were on salary. I turned to the crew and put the best face on and told them it was long overdue that we sat down together for a nice dinner. We all treated Rafaela the assistant to a fine meal. Bret was very apologetic but it wasn't his fault.

It turned out that Bret was soon booked for the Legends of Ring convention out here in New Jersey, so I reached out to Rafaela and Kirk the agent. We locked in a Friday night shoot in June, the night before the convention. Everything was good.

June soon came and so did Bret. We had the staff at the Crowne Plaza set up our breakout room with proper dining accouterments again, though Yogi's Sports Bar at the resort was handling the food. The Bistro at the Courtyard this was not. Bret would have eaten better back in February.

Bret arrived from the airport and joined us in the Middlesex Room. We all sat down around the long table and began eating as I waited for some questions from Bret about the show, or its format, or at least some of the events he'd come across in the shooting script I emailed Kirk that he wanted more details about. But he didn't say much. He asked me nothing. He didn't eat much, and if you've been to Yogi's then you know why. Finally, after a pretty quiet and awkward meal, I leaned back in my chair and asked Bret if he wanted to go through anything in advance.

"Like what?" he asked.

"Well, the format is a little unconventional, I realize," I said. "Sometimes the talent likes to ask about an event they came across in the shooting script that they don't remember. We could even show some video of the event if it was televised."

"What script?"

You fucking kidding me?

"Bret, how much did Kirk tell you about the project, about our *Timelines?*"

"Nothing."

I now had to tell Bret that he'd be painstakingly examining all the details of an entire year in his professional life, all of them having occurred 22 years ago, mind you. I know my initial reaction to this news was a little unseasoned.

"What?! I send him a goddamn script six months ago!"

"I never got it," he said. I leaned in and softened my tone and explained our series, and the year-by-year analysis of all the decisions of the company.

"This really sounds like something right up my alley," he said, perking up as much as Bret perks. Thank God he said that though. It allowed the blood to drain back into my body from my head. He wasn't intimidated by the concept in the least, and he was a fantastic guest.

The point of this story is that the innovation of the *Timeline* series depends entirely on the ability of the guest to recall the minutiae of the events and years we are covering. Can you tell me what you were thinking every day at work 22 years ago? I wanted Bret to do just that. And he did. But the heart of that series was in jeopardy because his agent didn't bother to give him a script or one iota of information regarding what we expected of him when he arrived on the set, other than ascertaining he wanted a grilled chicken salad.

Back when we first launched the *Timeline: The History of WWE* series, we were running a contest in conjunction with a pro wrestling website wherein free copies of one of our DVDs were given away. One of the winners was a worker in the media library of WWE and WWE Magazine. When I saw the address to which we were shipping the free DVD, Titan Tower, I dropped the winner an email. He was very complimentary and indicated his co-workers were big fans of ours. I had a bunch of our DVDs shipped to Titan Tower, in particular the entire *Timeline: The History of WWE* series to that point.

About six months later, *WWE Magazine* released an issue called "The History of WWE," and through the center of the entire magazine ran…you got it…a timeline. The historical events depicted in the magazine were told via text pop ups very much like the style of our onscreen timeline. My initial reaction was anger.

Then WWE announced their new John Morrison DVD would feature questions from the fans and he would answer them on-camera. Our most popular series at the time was *YouShoot,* featuring the unheard of concept of talent submitting to an interview comprised of fan questions. No one had ever done anything like this before us. I felt this was a final straw and, childishly, I got hot pissed.

I was forgetting the innovation arc, and I also sensed I was missing an opportunity. I spoke with Anthony and decided we had to do something with this. It was too obvious a theft for the penalty not to be called. We had to throw a flag somehow. We were in agreement that tact was needed here. There's nothing worse than a crybaby, bellowing to almost no one, "They stole from us!" We couldn't be that guy.

What we arrived at was a "Vince Loves KC" campaign. We created very funny artwork and launched the campaign which posited that with such blatant coincidences there was only one possible answer—the captain of the football team, Vince McMahon, the CEO of the billion dollar WWE, was secretly in love with little, ol' us! The tone of the campaign was very tongue-in-cheek, told as an unlikely love affair. It was hilarious and made the point, while positioning us accurately as a good-natured company that "gets it." There's a confidence that is exuded when dealing with an issue in such a fashion.

We even had a successful "Why Does Vince Love KC?" essay contest. We got tons of submissions and posted the top 10 on our site and sent the winners free DVDs. And some of the winning essays were absolutely hilarious. Our fans were writing fictional stories about Vince McMahon sweating our company. It was a very successful campaign that got us good press.

In the *Timeline: The History of WWE* example, as well as the TNA example, those responses to our product, which initially pissed me off, were actually just additional confirmation that we were innovators. We were advancing. It was also just the tip of the iceberg.

It will drive you mildly insane to have a slew of consistent copycats emulating your products. But there's a much healthier point of view in seeing that they are only answering your gunfire. They're only returning your fire because you are doing the right things. Now, move onto the next thing.

10. The Idea Is Not the Innovation

GENE SIMMONS LOOKED at me and smiled. I kept my cool, not letting the inner KISS mark explode to the surface. I wanted to be taken seriously—this was a pitch, and I knew I only had a few minutes. I never talked about this publicly before, but I was the creator of KISScream—the branded, frozen treats to be sold at venues across North America during the legendary band's summer 2004 tour.

Kayfabe Commentaries was not yet born and I was acting and working for a large investment bank on West 52nd Street in Manhattan. One night, jolted with inspiration, I sat at a graphics computer and designed a mock-up of ice cream cups. I knew the band would be doing a summer shed-tour, meaning hot, outside venues all season long. I used some KISS branded elements I stole from the Internet and adorned my revolution in rock n' roll frozen desserts with them.

I named the flavors: *Strutterfinger, Rocky Road All Nite,* and *King of the Nighttime Swirl.* Talk about a home run. I was the most excited person in the room, as my co-workers looked at me like an overgrown child, and my boss Dave was totally annoyed by this distraction to my paid duties. I pounded that bitch out until midnight and headed home with plans to hit FedEx the next morning.

I sent the proposal to Gene and waited for the call I knew would come. But after a couple of months, it hadn't. So I had to take this to Gene himself. I'd just finished reading his book *Sex Money KISS* and he touted the balls needed to support the entrepreneurial spirit he so valued. If anyone could understand a young, wide-eyed entrepreneur-at-heart jumping him and demanding an answer on that proposal, it was Gene. I'd get to him when he was in New York for his book tour.

Maybe he hadn't seen the KISScream papers. Some flunky probably tossed it aside, jealous they hadn't thought of it and brought it to Gene themselves. It was probably Tommy Thayer.

It was only a matter of weeks before Gene would probably sign a deal with me right on the spot. Would he need to partner Paul Stanley in on this decision for KISScream? Maybe he could get Paul on the phone right there and get his approval. Gene would probably fly me out to his house in L.A. to ink this as soon as he could. The summer tour was coming—we would need to get right into production sampling ingredients. Or maybe Tommy could handle that while Gene and I worked on some movie scripts in his home office.

I finally stood before Gene one spring afternoon downtown in Manhattan. I shook his hand and introduced him to my wife.

"Wife?" Gene said. "That is not a term I'm familiar with." Gene was proudly and publicly marriage-phobic, enhancing his image as a cocksman of the rock n' roll world.

"You should try it sometime," I said. I was nervous, but I knew I was done with small talk. I launched right into KISScream—the concept, the summer tour, the whole thing. I can't remember everything I said, but I know he was quick to try and cut me off.

"That's just an *idea*," he said. I didn't even listen. I plowed right through him.

"*Strutterfinger,* Gene." He smiled. "*King of the Nighttime Swirl!*" He actually chuckled at that. I stopped and threw open my outstretched hands—*what do you think?*

"Do you own an ice cream company?" he asked.

"No."

"Those are ideas," he reiterated. "Anyone can have an idea. 'I want to build the tallest building in the world.' Okay, great. How?"

"I don't know." And right there, the wind was out of my sails. I sounded like Butthead. "Uhhh…huh huh…I don't know." But it immediately made sense to me.

Your innovation has to follow through to execution. Innovation, despite common positioning, is not the creative idea. It may sound a little spiritual, but innovation is the concept-to-product thoroughfare of an idea previously unperfected and unconsidered, and the entire process therein. If you have a great idea but you can't do it, where is the innovation? When I'm sitting in traffic I sometimes fantasize about a car that can hover above the grind and fly me to my destination. Can't do anything about it though. Innovation? Nope. Crazy? Perhaps.

In the entertainment business, ideas are a dime-a-dozen. With the advent of digital video cameras and editing programs, it seems everyone is a "filmmaker" today. Every yo-yo that buys a camera is making a "film" now. (Ironically enough, none are being shot on film. They wouldn't know how.) And the reason that we're cursed with this proliferation of wannabe artistes is the misconception of the power of the idea.

Because of my background in film and TV, I've always been unfortunate enough to be on the receiving end of pitches and scripts from bankers, brokers, and the like. How does anyone feel justified in believing they can make a seamless entrée into a field that it took me years of college and even more years of professional participation to hone? I never sat in my doctor's office and said, "I'm gonna get me a stethoscope, lab coat, some gauze, and start treating patients." I have as about as many qualifications to make that proclamation as the banker that says, "I have a cool idea, I'm gonna make a film."

It's the fraudulent allure of "the idea." Great, you have an idea. You wanna make KISScream. Now what?

An idea is a sperm without an egg. Syd Field, the venerable screenwriting teacher and author, tells of the telltale sign of the professional screenwriter versus the amateur screenwriter—the amateur shields his script idea. He or she is always afraid to share their new idea, fearful that someone will steal their very original screenplay concept, in which a few people pull off a big heist, or some shit.

The experienced screenwriter knows that no matter who hears the idea for his or her screenplay, no one will be able to execute it like they can. The skill isn't in the *aha!* moment in the shower, but rather in the tireless work and artistry which brings that idea to life for the world. It's the compromises, the war against compromises, the production issues, the personality clashes, the glorious successes in the struggles that change our world—that's the magic of innovation.

How many truly original ideas exist anyway? Movies, TV shows, songs—most art is relatively derivative of something else nowadays. But that's okay because what you do with it is the only thing that matters.

Apple's iPods were just the Sony Walkman (for anyone under 30, they were those black boxes with headphones we put cassettes into and walked around listening to) in a digital form. Our show *Guest Booker* is just a talk show. *YouShoot* is just the last few minutes of a studio talk show, wherein the host takes the mic up into the crowd and the audience gets to ask the guest some questions. But what did Apple do with the Walkman? What did KC do with audience participation?

Apple took the idea and concept of the Sony Walkman and put a wheel on it, gave it a stylish makeover, added a linear menu system, and made your music digital. At KC we took the most provocative figures in pro wrestling, put them on *YouShoot,* and constructed the entire show with your emails and videos. I'm just there as ringmaster. We turned some of your questions into games. Innovation is in the crafting and the re-crafting.

Innovation is tied closely to The Blood—if you're a passionate participant in your market, you'll tell yourself what's needed in that market. You'll know it instinctively. An artist working on canvas everyday of their life will know what qualities are missing from that market and, upon opening their own business, will fill that need. Her canvasses will be well-stretched and perhaps the artist will develop a gizmo to aid them in the securing of the canvass to the frame. No market research is needed.

Now, as the product line develops, there may be some more research needed. Once the initial need is fulfilled there will likely be questions regarding the consumer's preference for certain options. The entrepreneurial artist will need to know what sizes of canvas are popular. She may prefer to work on smaller canvas, but she will need to know the demand for larger canvasses. The Blood will give life to great things, but it does not preclude the need for research.

The artist knows the companies that produce the best quality paint in her medium, which for this example we will assume is oil. But she may need to research acrylic. She will also need to research color. There's no doubt her shelves will be stocked with the best quality oil paint, but the preference of color is something that will be worth exploring. The artist prefers to work in earth tones, but she may discover a real consumer demand for primary colors. Maybe even more of a demand. So she will decide to stock their shelves with both earth tones and primary colors at a 40/60 ratio. Or maybe not. Maybe she will decide to position their company as a boutique shop, with a limited supply of only the finest lines of select items. It'll challenge her volume a bit. Hopefully the higher prices can make up for that.

At Kayfabe Commentaries we were passionate enough consumers in our market that we knew what programming was needed. There was plenty of trial and error, planning, and discussion, but we knew the void that sat in our market. *Guest Booker* took shoot-style programming to a whole new level. The allure of the first shoot-style interviews that hit the market in the mid-90s was in the voyeuristic peek we were getting into the once closed and protected world of pro wrestling. After years and years of peeking though, we needed even more exclusivity. How much further could we get inside?

Guest Booker was born out of that desire for more. We sought to take the sport's bookers (decision makers or writers for the sport) and delve into their creative process. In essence, we'd try and get further inside the business by having the architects themselves take us there. Then, through a booking exercise that's performed on every show, we see them demonstrate those skills in real time. It's akin to profiling the writers of *Friends* and then having them write an episode of *Star Trek*. We tape the process and allow you to witness how it all comes together.

The innovation of that series was born out of our passion for that programming—we identified what that segment needed but beyond that, market research was needed for insight into the preferences of our viewers. The decisions that helped us steer and shape the series as it developed were made entirely from listening to the viewing preferences of our fans. Initially the booking exercises were a sizable portion of the first episodes. But we were seeing reviews and feedback that were largely critical of the success and feasibility of the booker's exercise. So we felt we needed to spend less time on the booking exercise and more time profiling the booker's mind and his philosophy.

Guess what the feedback was? "Where's all the booking?"

We then had to deal with a segment of viewers who felt cheated that they weren't seeing a bunch of actual booking. The market research showed a conflicting message—too bland and too spicy at the same time. We realized the magic would be in a special blend of the two, and that's what we developed for future *Guest Bookers*.

So the innovation is born in The Blood. The market and your passionate knowledge of it, and participation in it, will guide your product to glory. Just listen to it. And if the consumers feel version 2.0 needs a smaller handle, put it on.

11. Differentiation is a Promise

AT KC WE seek to distinguish ourselves from other production companies in the wrestling space in more ways than just the kind of programming we produce. When you are a guest on a KC show, we want you to have a First Class experience. Earlier I mentioned the lengths to which we went during the Bret Hart edition of *Timeline.* I know how some of these guys and gals are treated by promoters and production companies in our space, and our differentiation from them is important. The vast majority of the time we succeed.

One of the times we flew Vince Russo out to shoot with us, I had to entrust a third party with Vince's pickup from the airport and delivery to our set. I was tied up shooting other shows and

Vince would be landing in Newark in late afternoon. I knew another promoter had talent doing airport runs, so I asked if he could have someone handle Vince. We would be doing that promoter's show the following evening, so it was pertinent to his indie federation's business as well.

I was between shoots when I got a call from Vince, who had just landed.

"Bro, are you here?" he asked. I told him I wasn't but the promoter had dispatched one of his young wrestlers to pick up Vince. Last text I saw from him said he would meet Vince by baggage.

A few minutes go by and my phone rings again.

"Bro, there's no one here," Russo says.

"I just saw a text from the kid, he's coming in the terminal now. Just hang for a minute, he'll get to you."

Two minutes later.

"Bro…there ain't *no one* here." I'm dying. I guess the kid had to get gas or something so he got there a little late. I didn't know the kid, but this indie promoter was bringing in talent all the time. I had no reason to doubt he'd be able to arrange a pickup.

I got a text saying the kid sees Russo. I call him.

"He should be right there, Vince. He sees you."

"Bro, I still don't see anyone. Oh, hang on…okay he's here." With a sigh, I tell the crew Vince is on his way and we should grab a bite at Yogi's. I'll now be able to eat without a stomach ache, as the talent is secured and on his way.

Not five minutes goes by and I'm getting a call from Russo again. Flat tire? Lost? What now?

"Bro, this guy has no windshield wipers and it's pouring outside. I'm making him pull over—can you send someone else?"

I was fit to be tied. We'd worked with Vince before so I wasn't worried about first impressions, but we still always wanted a top-notch experience with our guests and I didn't know if it was Vince being a prima donna or if this kid was as mentally challenged as was being proposed.

"I'm coming. Tell me where you are."

"He's pulling into a gas station." Vince gave me the address of the station just off the N.J. Turnpike in Elizabeth. I told the team to enjoy dinner and I stormed out of the hotel and into my car. In minutes I was on the Turnpike North, heading from Monroe to Elizabeth, about a half-hour ride, possibly even more due to the downpour. I just wanted to get there and tell this kid what an idiot he was.

Well, I couldn't. When I arrived at the gas station flagged in my GPS, there was no other car waiting. It was really coming down outside and I looked around thinking I may have landed in a gas station across the street from where I was supposed to be. No, this was the one—seemingly dropped in the middle of a knot of highways onramps, offramps, and jam packed, flooded roads during metropolitan area rush hour. What the hell?

Finally I pulled my car past the pumps and there, inside the little convenience store, leaning on the window with his suitcase, was Vince Russo. The former head writer for WWE, WCW, and TNA, was leaning on the glass, looking like a wayward hitchhiker. The fucking kid didn't even wait with him! He pulled into a gas station, dropped Russo off in a torrential downpour, and left.

I jumped out and headed to the store as Russo came out. I was beyond apologetic and tried to grab his bag and carry it, like some youngboy in Japan. Wasn't that some sign of wresting respect? I don't know. I seem to remember hearing "carrying my bags" used as a pecking order thing. Well, that night I was beyond embarrassed and probably would have carried Vince himself if I could.

"I got it, bro, I got it," he said as I grabbed for his suitcase. We dodged puddles and finally made it inside my car. Vince was good natured about it—I'm sure he's seen it all in his years, and he already knew that our company rolled a little differently than had been shown that day. He knew there was a true differentiation between KC and others in our field.

Once Vince knew that his original driver wasn't associated with us in any way, he told me the full story. The kid had garbage piled in the backseat so high that the rear window wasn't even visible. Imagine being sent to the airport to pick up a celebrity and being okay with that situation? Being a slob is one thing, but being so clueless is quite another.

While they were driving, the rain and chilly air was causing a fair amount of fogging on the windshield. That, coupled with the water streaming down, made for impossible visibility. This numb nuts grabs a rag—

"...Bro, a freakin' *rag...*"

—and rolls down his window, reaches outside, and starts wiping off the windshield from the outside *as he drives on the New Jersey Turnpike in rush hour!* Vince asked him about the wipers and was told they didn't work. I then understood why Vince asked to be dropped off. He would've been killed before he got to Exit 12.

Later when I spoke with the promoter about the debacle he did confirm the kid was a bit of a shithead. I thanked the promoter for choosing him for me. He then told me his locker room was little upset that Vince was being brought in. Some workers were threatening to not work at the show.

"You kidding me?" I said. "They make $50 a show. And they're making threats?"

"I told them it was you bringing him in and not me. So they're gonna wrestle."

"Jesus, thank God," I said. "You would've really been screwed without Hulk Hogan working your Rahway Recreation Center show." Not sure if he appreciated the sarcasm, but this news about his unhappy locker room was A.) the stupidest thing I'd ever heard from an indie wrestling company and B.) a sideways justification for treating my guest less than professionally. It illustrates the particular species of bottom feeder that permeates the independent wrestling scene.

It should be rather obvious that differentiation is not difficult for us as far as talent relations is concerned. We always treated our talent very differently than competitors. But all of that is invisible to the consumer. Your reputation within your industry is important because, though you may not specifically deal with talent in your Business of Blood, you'll probably have vendors, suppliers, and a dozen other relationships you need to maintain. Just be reliable in your business practices and that'll probably differentiate you from many of your competitors.

However, the most obvious and important form of differentiation with which you'll be concerned is in your market, for your customers. There are a lot of options out there for any product, service, or show. You want people to choose yours, so you have to go about creating a reason for that.

As you're considering why anyone would want to visit your business, you have to introduce the extension to that question which is, "...with all these other businesses standing beside mine?" The question is really "How will we be noticed?" In the physical sense, there's marketing and advertising, which we'll delve into. But these practices only get a business *seen*. That's a little different from being noticed. You actually need someone to walk into your store, whether virtual or brick and mortar, and have their experience be memorable.

Don't discount the "memorable" part of that. Once they're inside, you're not out of the woods—you still run the risk of not being noticed. In a store of any kind, the décor, pricing, products, lighting, music, and the overall shopping experience will paint a definitive picture. How much distinguishability is there really from clothing store to clothing store? The ones that do show a strong and unique differentiation are probably the most successful stores.

In Seth Godin's amusing book *The Purple Cow*, he uses that very mental image to illustrate that getting noticed starts with differentiation. He tells a tale of a long drive wherein the cow fields all begin to blur in our eyesight after a time—until we see a purple cow, that is. Its novelty certainly makes one take notice and start talking to the other people in the car.

The spirit of Godin's fable is certainly accurate—one must work to distinguish their company and brand. But there's an inherent promise in that differentiation. That cow has given us some subtle expectations. The cow's milk might be purple. It also could taste like grape. There's an expectation in seeing a purple cow, if it is to be a fully realized experience. It should fulfill its big promise, or else it is only a freakish defect. The only thing that's truly unique is the coat of hair. (Fur? Gotta brush up on my animal science.)

A product's differentiation has to come in the fulfillment of its promise. A quick, :15 second television promo for an NBA basketball game will likely show the stars of the teams that will meet—say the Lakers and Celtics—making remarkable shots, blocks, and dunks. The promo ends with a triumphant, fists raised shot of some players. We're also given the air date and time of the game on that network.

What are the promises they've made to us? Firstly, we're promised that we'll see the Lakers play the Celtics if we tune in. Secondly, we are promised marquee stars on both teams that will be playing in that game, and they're capable of the impressive shots, blocks, and dunks that keep you and me on the couch, and them on NBA hardwood. We're then shown a triumphant ending shot with fists raised, guaranteeing us that there will be a winner. Lastly, the date and time guarantee that we'll be able to see this game if we clear our appointments for that evening, or at least set the DVR.

The NBA and the television network must now fulfill all those promises. But if we tune in at 8 o'clock that night and the two last place teams were playing instead of the Celtics and Lakers, dropping passes and missing shots all over the place, we'd have an unfulfilled promise. They showed the Lakers and Celtics in the promo in an effort to woo us. Further, if the promo never explicitly said "Lakers versus Celtics" but instead said just, "NBA Basketball" but they showed only those two teams, there's an implied promise. If they tricked us into tuning in, we most certainly aren't going to continue watching, and we'll probably discard any of those future NBA promos for that network. They may have shown us a purple cow in the promo, but the milk is ordinary and we're going to view the differentiation as a defect.

When Vince Russo first left TNA after having written for wrestling companies since the mid 90s, we snagged him for a live show. We had the *YouShoot: LIVE* model in effect since we did an episode with Dixie Carter, the head of TNA Wrestling. Since *YouShoots* open up the questioning to the fans, we saw that we could do episodes with live audiences, wherein people would question the lighting rods we intended to feature, in person.

We flew Vince out to shoot some promos after announcing the show, and they went well. One of the promos we shot featured a short, sit down interview with me and him. Though the humorous, scripted promos we shot were fun, Anthony and I knew we needed to address what everyone would be thinking when they heard about this show. So we decided to ask him those questions pointedly, on camera. I asked him what he expected from the show. I asked him if he would be honest and name names. We wanted to let the fans know he wasn't going to play nice and hold back after seeing his name set aflame for the previous 15 years.

We ran all the promos but the murmurs persisted, same as the ones from Dixie's shoot—"He won't bury anyone." "They won't ask hard questions." On and on and on. The thing that always floored me was that I was *brutal* to Dixie with fan questions and videos for her *YouShoot LIVE*. But that truth was ignored and the basement trolls reported we went soft on her. You can't win.

But two things happened that proved the Internet trolls correct in the Vince Russo case—he didn't name names, and the live audience was loaded with Russo marks. I mean loud, boisterous defenders of Vince and his product. At one point we had to have security ask the front row to quiet down. No one in the house confronted him with anything that could have sparked some interesting debate. We invited the press to join us in person or via Internet. No one of note did.

We'd failed to keep our promise. I was sitting on the stage across from him and when he said, "I don't wanna call him out" about someone, and I died inside. I was suddenly a fan watching this at home, and I was annoyed. This was the most controversial figure in the sport at the time. Our live iPPV was laying an egg. At least New Jack showed up and asked a question.

Differentiation carries with it a huge responsibility to fulfill the promise. As consumers, we'll even pay a premium for a fulfilled promise if it is advertised consistently. If an upscale restaurant moves onto the strip with a unique façade, soft ambient music, fashionably dressed staff, tasteful low light, and a minimalist menu and the food matches the promise, we will leave feeling fulfilled. We probably paid a premium price to eat at a restaurant like that, but if that promise was fulfilled and the experience is deemed wholly accurate, the price was justified.

At Kayfabe Commentaries, our differentiation comes in the uniqueness of our programming, quality of our shows, and our commitment to customer service. Russo ducked the questions at the live show, yes. But I'm cutting us a break on that one. There was no way for us to know how he'd answer. He's since made up for that by doing some great, insightful programming like his two editions of *Timeline* and his *Guest Booker.*

The concepts behind our shows are like none you've ever seen in the shoot market. If we only had that differentiation but we didn't deliver on our promise, a customer would put in our show, see a product with sub-par production values, a lame concept, a bad interviewer, and they'd be done with us. Further, if the DVD took four weeks to arrive, or if they contacted us with a question about our streaming service and we didn't respond for two days, that would also challenge our ability to earn their business on a consistent basis. But our promise is as important to us as our differentiation. Yes, we loved lighting the world on fire with bold concepts like *Guest Booker, YouShoot,* and *Timeline*, but we also place strenuous emphasis on fulfilling our promise of high production values and amazing service.

It all goes back to The Blood. As passionate fans, we knew that a fair segment of the shoot interview industry suffered from poor production values, a lack of conceptual ingenuity, and lackluster customer service. I have yet to meet a KC customer that felt we didn't fulfill our promise as we differentiated ourselves from the pack. You may not have liked what a particular guest on a *Guest Booker* did for the booking exercise, but I guarantee you that you've never seen a show like it. Further I guarantee that it was shot, mic'ed, lit, scored, hosted, and edited to broadcast quality, and also that it arrived at your house quickly. (Outside the U.S., give us a week or so. A German customer told me that our DVDs arrive to his house before mail order items from within Germany. That stuff gets me psyched.)

Take a second and think about the greats in your life—your favorite products, favorite athlete, a great lover. They have all differentiated themselves from the pack somehow, but they've also delivered on their promise. If they hadn't, you would have stopped using the products, wearing their jersey, or dating them.

12. Personalization

THIS BLOOD BOND between customer and company has its roots in their shared passion. Beyond that, the strengthening and reinforcement comes from the production of great product. But there's also a subtle, psychological element that puts lots of weight in the customer experience. Ask yourself how much personalization your company has. Do your customers know they're dealing with actual people when they have points of contact with your company? For all the talk of automation these days, one should tread carefully when it comes to customer service. It's one of the few touches you have with your customers. Don't screw it up.

There's nothing more frustrating than being treated like a

commodity. We kind of expect this impersonal treatment from mass-market suppliers, like your cell phone company or health insurance provider. But a Business of Blood has been built on the premise of community and kinship. A Business of Blood has that insight into the fan's mind. We should know better. We can't expect them to take to the streets for us on the one hand, and expect to depersonalize them on the other.

Social media makes personalization very easy today. It doesn't mean you have to engage with every tweet or Facebook post. You probably couldn't, and you'd be answering the same questions multiple times. Fans need to scroll down every once and a while. Kayfabe Commentaries has a Facebook page and a Twitter feed. Posts and tweets from those accounts deal with company issues, teasers of upcoming shows, behind the scenes photos, and anything our company wants to bring to mass market eyes.

My personal Twitter feed is a different story. That's where I'll post things that I, not my company, want to share with you. In the quest for personalization, don't have your company sharing political views or photos of your dinner. That's for your personal Twitter or Facebook accounts.

Your personalization starts with your product and that's actually the easiest part. We've already established that your passion for this field has created that sense of awareness and insight into your customers. The Blood grants you that all-important initial bond. That's a huge point of contact, that touch. The next touch is usually when the package arrives, when they get it home, or when the service is performed. So be quick about shipping and appointments if that's your business.

At Kayfabe Commentaries we go to great lengths to ensure our customer service is remarkable. That's a major touch for us.

While every company talks about customer service being important, they really mean customer service should be convenient for them, not necessarily the customer. Automated or outsourced customer service takes a real gamble with that important touch. In many cases, it destroys it. I get physically ill when I have to reach out to a company for whom I was a patron. I know the runaround is about to begin. It blows.

Today you even see companies use a system that, upon receiving you customer service email, generates an automated email reply that appears to have been written by a person. But if you read carefully you can see that it's automatically generated, triggered by a few keywords and phrases in your initial support email. The reply partially addresses what you've written about but it never fully answers the question. In some cases I've just been directed to a FAQ page or even a forum on a website, which I have already scoured for my answer, to no avail. If I've taken the time to write a three paragraph explanation of this issue I'm having with your product, don't send me, "Maybe this is what you're looking for...otherwise go look for the answer yourself here." That's what I hear in those autoreplies. That sucks.

Hey, let's be honest here—are some customers ridiculous? Oh my Lord. If I asked Brian from shipping to write this chapter it might never end. He loves emails asking where the DVD is that was ordered yesterday. Hey, we understand you guys like our stuff. But give the post office a chance.

Then there are the pissed off emails about WWN moving their login screen, making it tougher to get in and watch our OnDemand programming. We help as much as we can, but we aren't WWN. We're not DIY Wrestling who handle our download sales. We don't want to send you away without an answer, so we'll get on the site and try and help with locations and the like. But guys, we can't handle technical support for a website we don't own. They're vendors. We shoot the shows.

Internet business marketers love to tout the merits of automation—citing these efficient ways to handle customer service. Our Business of Blood has a very different goal than those overnight entrepreneurs. We are seeking to build an army of dedicated and loyal warriors. We are looking to forge a bond that will last a lifetime. Our relationship with our fans is built at an emotional level, while these other Internet marketers are short-sighted, concerned with only convenience—and as a result, any devotion on the part of a customer is not a devotion to that cold company, but rather to only product and price. And when the company across the street produces it more cheaply, guess what? Exactly. The bond with their company is not a bond with the company at all.

The good news is that as a start-up Business of Blood, you will not have the volume of customer service emails that you and a helper or two will not be able to address. Answer them personally, address the problem as soon as you can, fix it somehow, and offer a follow-up option like, "If that doesn't work, please write us back and let us know."

We generally get a few types of customer service emails at KC—a lost or late package, which we can track easily for the customer via USPS; a programming question or suggestion; or a big ol' thank you email. We respond to each of them with equal vigor. If someone took the time out of their day to tell you they're happy or unhappy about something, then that means your company is quite important to them. That deserves a personal response. Not just a response…a *personal* response. All of these interactions are opportunities. They are touches with your customers, after all. It's yet another opportunity to solidify your brand promise to them, and if you're thinking the right way, to give them a little something extra.

At KC we offer our customers a few opportunities for touches. For a long time we maintained a message board at a partner website called Kayfabe Memories, before social media replaced message boards. On the board, fans discussed releases, asked me questions, and even posted questions for *YouShoots*. The discussion on this forum was often invigorating and challenging and I enjoyed going on and answering all the fans' questions about the company and anything else they came up with. We also had Jason Hart, son of the late booker Gary Hart, hosting a forum on our board. Jason fielded all questions about his brilliant father who had a memorable appearance on our show *Guest Booker*. This kind of personalization keeps our fans in direct contact with us and also adds some value to the customer experience.

Through our forum and our activity on Twitter and Facebook, we were able to maintain meaningful and informative touches with our fans. Using these outlets for a series of shills for your product will get pretty tiresome, pretty quickly for your customers. These outlets will not be looked upon favorably by anyone with whom you wish to engage if the conversation is only one-way. You're not there to sell, per se. Many message boards didn't even allow you to shill and would suspend your account for doing so. But most will allow you to place some art in the signature of your posts, and that art should definitely be a graphic which links to your website. This was a great, free tool to market our wares, especially early on. We did this voraciously when we launched. It was a huge part of our marketing. It took a massive time commitment, but the price was right.

Message boards and social networks really hate shilling. It's top-down marketing (more later) and that is the antithesis of the tenets upon which social media has been built. The global Internet community and all its tools were founded on bottom-up philosophy. Don't take that lightly.

On Twitter and Facebook, if you are on there as your company rather than an individual, and you've told people to follow you on these social nets, then you can disseminate product info there. It's likely that your followers have agreed to follow you on there for exactly that kind of information. They already get the cat videos from their mom. Ensure there's some added value for customers and fans to sign up. Offer them an advantage, perhaps. At KC, when we had a limited-run item, like our popular and rare Signature Edition DVDs, wherein the star of the show autographs a replica disc to be framed and displayed, we'd announce the sale of these limited run items on Facebook, Twitter, and our email list first. They often sold out very quickly to these followers. That's an advantage of staying in close contact with us via these social nets and our mailing list.

Our programming also has fan-centric elements too, which tie all of this together. Our popular series *YouShoot* features all of the questions being asked by fans submitted via email, webcam, and our social media outlets. If you posted one, you may have had yours asked.

Our show *Wrestling's Most* was a countdown show in which the fans voted on a particular topic that was tabulated, counted down, and commented on by stars of the ring. The fan, our customer, has a huge stake in our programming, and ultimately, our business. That's the ultimate partnership that yields ultimate brand loyalty.

But if you open up to the public you will have to deal with what the public has to say. You need to read the criticism, both justified and ridiculous alike, and understand it's part of the price paid for the passionate engagement with fans.

On Facebook, our fans can post reviews and comments on our titles that other fans can see and join in on the discussion. These outlets feature meaningful content and we really do view these social networks as added value for our fans more than anything. We always work to give our Kayfabe Commandos, as they've come to be known, a greater KC experience. And you should start to think in those terms also, and figure out how your business can be an experience.

We were very close to producing a series called *House Show,* where a star of the wrestling business would spend the day at a fan's house and we'd film it. We solicited entries for the first editions of the show, and if you wanted Kamala, Val Venis, or The Iron Sheik in your house chilling with the family for the day, you could send us an email. Talk about bringing our shows to the fans. We had these fantastic images in our heads of Sheiky working the grill in an apron, maybe Grandma sitting on Val Venis's lap.

We ultimately scrapped the series when we could not legally insure ourselves against some liability if something happened to a fan or a star. We love that personalization we've built with our Commandos and we don't want any hurt or killed. That should probably be a priority of yours as well.

House Show isn't alone as far as shows that never saw the light of day, though most weren't announced like *House Show.* Hell, some weren't even discussed outside the KC sets, but served as a fine source of amusement and fantasy for us. And I don't necessarily think they were all bad ideas—I would have loved to watch some of these, irrespective to profitability.

How about another countdown? Here are the **Top 5 KC Ideas for Shows We Just Couldn't Bring Ourselves to Shoot**:

#5 - *Tuesdays with Orndorff* - Not sure if that would've been the title, but it's a damn good one. Ever wonder what it would be like to accompany "Mr. Wonderful" Paul Orndorff on an average day? Well, this show would've been for you. Imagine a cinema verite style journey with Paul as he does some grocery shopping, gets a haircut, and does whatever the day requires. Wouldn't be wrestling, or anything like that—strictly a slice-of-life portrait of Orndorff. Anthony pitched it, as he did most of this list, and we would have been marks for it. But it would never generate significant, single-release sales.

#4 - *Therapy* - We didn't have a title for this but it was to be an actual, 50-minute psychotherapy session with a licensed psychologist. We wanted The Iron Sheik to be the first guest, but as soon as we cooked up the idea, Howard Stern started doing a show on his Sirius channel called *Meet the Shrink*. He had members of his wack pack in recorded therapy sessions, which was basically our idea.

Truthfully, I thought this was a little exploitative. (Ya think?) If anything very private and damaging were ever revealed I think I'd regret airing it. Maybe I wouldn't have. Either way, I felt like a dirtbag approaching doctors with the idea.

#3 - *YouShoot: From Beyond* - It's me, a psychic medium, and a Ouija board, getting answers to all your questions from guests in the afterlife. I imagined you would have had a lot to ask Randy

Savage, Curt Hennig, and Professor Toro Tanaka, and this could have been your chance. But the problem here would have been authenticity. No psychic could have faked this. Unless it was a real communication from the other side, no purported medium could sustain exhaustive questioning, answering as Ivan Koloff the entire time.

Was there a big part of me interested in seeing how this would play out? Yes. But for the most part, I don't believe in the ability of anyone to talk to the dead, though if you watched me interview Chyna you could make a case for it. She was allegedly alive at the time of the taping.

More so than the fact that I thought the show would be a work, was that I was struggling with the ethics. I have a very broad gradient in what I would classify as entertainment, but this was hazy. It was probably poor taste.

#2 - *Ribs* - Who doesn't love a good rib story? Ribs, or pranks, have been a part of the pro wrestler's lifestyle on the road for decades. I've been around enough of the workers to hear them all. Mr. Fuji, Mr. Perfect Curt Hennig, Dynamite Kid, and Owen Hart were commonly believed to be some of the masters of such chicanery. I would have loved to ask them all about it on *YouShoot: From Beyond.* Maybe we should have gone with the show.

For the living pranksters of the business, we would have had the show *Ribs,* wherein the workers sat and exchanged their best rib stories, while eating ribs. See what we did there? Gigantic plate, heaping with saucy spare ribs, while Don Muraco, The Honky Tonk Man, and JJ Dillon sat gnashing bones and licking their fingers, talking about pad locking someone's gym bag to water pipe in a Boston Garden locker room. This was a brainchild of Anthony's, one he enjoyed telling me was a sure-thing. I wasn't sure he was serious, and was less sure of its potential.

#1 - *Ox in a Box* - Here's Anthony's finest unfilmed creation. The concept is simple—Ox Baker in a hotel room, being taped by small, surveillance cameras. That's it. What does he do all day and night? What would he order from room service? What does he watch on TV? Sports? Classic editions of *I Love Lucy?*

I don't think it was ever an attempt to catch anything salacious or shocking. It was the normalcy of it that would have been entertaining as giant, scary Ox Baker plodded around the room like your grandfather might. But it's Ox Baker. Shortly after cooking this one up, Ox ended up in a permanent box, and that was that.

13. Negotiation

ONE NIGHT I was preparing to negotiate an offer for a real estate client who was also a friend of mine. I was preparing him for what was likely to come, and for how the jousting was likely to play out. This was the part of real estate that people seemed to both love, and also become bristly about. It is *always* a bit contentious, and *always* personal. When negotiations begin, it is no longer a product or a property being sold. From the perspective of the seller, the buyer is putting a price on the memories and hard work that their property represents to them. In the mind of the buyer, the seller thinks they're an asshole who will try and rip them off because they're desperate.

There are entire books written on the psychology of

negotiation. I've read some. I'm not sure what I was looking for, perhaps something to ease the uncomfortable process of *you go high, I'll go low,* and the spectrum of emotions that ensues.

As my real estate client sat there, ready to start this process for his first property, he asked, "Why does it have to be a game?"

I was taken aback. I started to answer—I'm sure I gave some explanation about my being contracted to look after his interests, while the seller and their agent are looking out for theirs, so there's a process, and blah, blah, blah. But I couldn't get the poignancy of his innocent question out of my mind.

Why the game? Why are we starting *here* in our offer…only to go *there* in a week? Why are the sellers listing *there* in price…knowing they'll be coming down *here?* There are a ton of reasons, and I know them all, but none of them are good. Why, like Dave asked me, go through the game?

We've become accustomed to accepting that this is the de-facto process for purchasing in certain situations. We don't walk into the department store and begin negotiating the price of the item on the shelf. It has to be priced correctly by the store, or it won't move. If there's any negotiation, it's internal as we decide whether or not the item is worth its sticker, or if we can afford it.

So again, why the game? Regardless of the reasons, the underlying question cannot be ignored, and that is, "Can we eliminate the game?" Can we participate in no-game negotiations? Better still, are we strong enough to turn any negotiations, despite the actions of the other party, into no-game negotiations?

Obviously we can. You will be the better businessperson for subjecting yourself to this grueling process of killing the game, and the sense of empowerment is so very worth it. Your decisions will have so much more clarity. The process of eliminating the game takes discipline, and adhering to it takes even more still. And it starts with you.

Entering the no-games negotiation with conviction is a must. I don't mean faux confidence or arrogance. There is no real strategy, and there is no overabundance of thought. What you should be practicing is a total release of desire—perhaps a Zen state would be a good model. You will enter the process with just knowledge, and conviction…calm, cool conviction. Such conviction has been fostered by the myriad research and homework you've done before entering the no-games negotiation session. If your processes were correct and your numbers accurate, you will use them to get you into the open, Zen state.

The best model I have for the no-games negotiation is that of shopping for shoes. Don't laugh. This model will deliver you the discipline if you return to it. I wear a size 9 shoe. It does not change based on circumstantial events. It does not change based on the passion and sales tactics of the shoe salesperson. It doesn't change on the attractiveness of the shoe designs available to me. I'm a 9. This will not change. When I enter the shoe store, I am looking for the 9. If they are not selling 9 shoes, I am out the door rather quickly. Can they realistically sell me an 11? How hilarious would that negotiation process be?

You are shopping for shoes in negotiation. You need a 9, or whatever shoe size you wear. That dispassionate fact should permeate your attitude. If it doesn't fit, then it doesn't fit. Perhaps there are very tiny modifications you can make. I have added soft padding to shoes to get to a 9 $^{1}/_{2}$ when they don't make the style in a 9. But that's a small concession, and it's only a concession I have made when my size isn't available. I'd never pad a size 9 $^{1}/_{2}$ when I know the seller has a size 9.

Knowing your shoe size in a business negotiation comes from doing good homework and planning. Sometimes there's a great deal of research needed to arrive at the knowledge that you're a size 9. But once you do, the entire scenario needs to be reframed in your mind to that of a shoe store.

That framing should put you in a good mindset, and should be a big boost in getting you the conviction necessary for the process, which has now been greatly simplified for you. During the discussions with the other party, keep returning to this model and replacing the details with the shore store. Are they selling you an 11? Then you need to leave. But in order to do so you must have the conviction to walk away as well. Remember, a shoe that doesn't fit is a waste anyway. There's another one out there that does fit. Go find it.

My example of *The Great Debate '08* is size 9 versus size 11 scenario. The show was priced at 11 and I probably should have walked, unless I found a way to make my size 11 for that show—but this was before entering the iPPV realm and we weren't doing Signature Editions yet. I'd imagine the collector would have paid a pretty penny for an edition of the show signed by both Bruno and Harley.

The research you'll be conducting to find your shoe size will be the foundation of your decisions regarding this no-games negotiation. It's imperative that you use accurate data and projections. That's not even really the hard part, truth be told. The real difficulty is in accepting these numbers as fact with such conviction, that you're able to achieve that Zen-like placidity and never question your decision to walk away. You wouldn't think twice walking away from the shoe store if they didn't sell your size.

If there's a part of you fearing being seen as inflexible, don't worry about that. Are you inflexible because you won't cram your foot in a size 7? Be polite in negotiation, but stay firm in your decision and be thorough in your explanation as to why something will not work for you. Don't be a dick and say things like "final offer" and alienate yourself from future negotiations with that party. Chances are they'll come back later. Having established yourself as a smart businessperson who adheres to a budget will help you when they return. People will realize you're someone who knows what they want and doesn't play games.

There may be some concessions to be made, and that's fine, as long as it fits in with your shoe size. But you'll know whether or not it does or doesn't in advance, or at the very least your gut will tell you when you hear the offer or counter offer. You likely know that there are some shoe companies that make their wares a little bigger, so a size lower may be a perfect fit in that case. Perhaps you have to go down to an 8 for that style of shoe, but it's not too tight and you'll break them in after wearing them for a week or so. The key is that the shoe *fits.* If the number slides a bit, that concession is fine if you leave with a shoe that you can wear.

At KC, when I am made aware of a wrestler's availability I usually make the first offer. Sometimes I'll feel Anthony out on where he thinks the price tag should be for that talent and for that particular show. After Anthony and I confer and make sure we have some programming into which they fit and a place on the schedule for it, I'll reach out to the talent, the agent, or promoter acting as the intermediary. If the talent is someone with whom we've worked before, the process is usually pretty quick and easy.

Because Anthony and I have discussed our collective shoe size and agreed to it, the process of no-games negotiation is quick and painless. One way or the other.

I'm sometimes asked who is more difficult to work with—the old school wrestling legends or the new generation of wrestler. There's no set rule, as far as which is more difficult. Some are great to deal with, some are not. Some negotiations are easy, and some have flaws. In negotiation, both generations of wrestler have separately unique flaws.

Mind you, the great majority of our discussions go off without a hitch. But I find that the ones that don't go well usually fail for a couple of particular reasons. The first scenario is a negotiation with the legend that is out of touch with the marketplace and their place in it, and the second is the modern wrestler that is out of touch with who they are. They're easy to recognize and even easier to walk away from. One is a size 7 and the other is a size 11. Remember, I'm a 9.

Quite a few years ago we were approached by Super Agent Eric Simms about the availability of WWE legend George "The Animal" Steele. He didn't really fit into any of the series we had back at that time, but we did have a concept for an investigative special that he would have been able to do.

I'd always wanted to probe the life of the wrestling road agent. In a layman's example, back in the glory days of the sport they were the on-site supervisor at each arena. They fined late wrestlers, settled disagreements, ensured the matches went as prescribed, and reported all goings-on back to the office. It was a thankless and fascinating job. I thought a peek inside that job would be right up our fans' alley, and George was a road agent in the late 80s.

Simms told us up front what Steele's fee would be. There was another shoot producer already committed to doing a project with him and they'd agreed to this fee. I wouldn't move beyond our offer, which was about 20% below what Eric quoted me. I told him that was it—that was our price. I'd seen George interviewed before and he's a great piece of talent. He would be very interesting. But for us, a title released under the investigative special umbrella is a bit of a risk because it doesn't have the advantage of being an episode of an existing, multi-edition series that already has an established fan base. We can predict a sales baseline for a title like that. An investigative special will perform on the weight of a.) KC's reputation, which will certainly get the ball rolling; b.) the size and attractiveness of the name attached to it, which in this case was marginal already, and would be further marginalized by the fact that we knew another producer would be releasing a title with him; and c.) the concept of the show, which was good, but rather narrow.

This was a risk, but if we got Steele at a bargain and could block-book the production (shoot multiple shows in the same day and same location to amortize expenses over several shows), it would work.

The talent's rate didn't work for us. The shoe size for this show was a 9. Given the price for George, the shoe being displayed was a 10 plus—an easy pass. Simms did his best at his assigned task, working on behalf of the talent. He reinforced the great stories this man had to tell. I whole-heartedly agreed with him. He would be a great interview. And it's a shame he wouldn't lower his rate to meet our price. And still, I pass.

"But you know where I am if anything changes," I said. "Let me know who else you have down the road, buddy." Done. No games. No enmity. Everyone leaves with his dignity, and everyone's shoes still fit.

Some of the more modern-era talent are a different animal. Wrestlers of yesteryear, like George Steele and his contemporaries, wanted to be just that—wrestlers. Today, many young men and women do this as an entree to mainstream entertainment, or so they think. There are the extremely rare exceptions to the failure of the pro wrester to cross over, like The Rock and Steve Austin. These guys are incredibly charismatic and hit the lottery by being able to be as captivating on the big screen as they were in the ring and in promos. Can't teach that stuff. And 99.9% of people don't have it.

Yet 99.9% of the young talent I talk to say things about "their career" and you best believe they're not talking about their wrestling career. They see it as one big life in the public eye—in the ring, in movies and TV, and music. But they won't have one. I've been in the mainstream entertainment business for over 20 years, on both sides of the camera. Professional wrestling carries with it zero respect in the entertainment business. As a matter of fact, it will be a strike *against* someone walking into an agent's office proclaiming they'll be a star because they are a big deal…in wrestling! I guess if WWE's movie division keeps cranking out versions of *The Marine* there will always be some film work for them. But outside of the insular wrestling sphere, not so much.

Though I know this, many of the stars today do not. So their price always comes in very high once they are released from one of the big wrestling federations. They're free of the restrictive contracts of WWE or TNA or wherever, and they prepare to get top dollar on the independent circuit. I happily pass on them. I know by waiting two years, as the dreams of record sales and movie roles fade, they'll be available at half the price. Reality does my negotiating in these instances. All I have to say is, "No, thank you," and it's easier to do when you see the sales figures of modern era wrestlers for shoot programming. Our financial statements are probably the only place Brutus Beefcake out drew Alberto Del Rio 3-to-1.

I don't want to sound like I'm hostile toward the younger talent, and there is certainly a percentage that would be happy wrestling on the road forever. But it's a very small percentage who actually want to be a wrestler forever. It's really not these kids' fault. They're in a wrestling business now that desperately tries to posit itself as "sports entertainment" and make far-reaching attempts in the areas of movie production, football leagues, and other mainstream media. The wrestling is basically the same, the attractions are basically the same, and the fans are basically the same. The only ones that think they're different are the people in the wrestling company.

The epilogue of the George "The Animal" Steele story is that he was again offered to us a couple of years later. We now had a series in which he would fit—*Timeline: The History of WWE*. We could give him the year 1986 to profile, as he was pretty prevalent on TV working with Randy "Macho Man" Savage in an Elizabeth love angle. I returned Eric Simms's call and named my price and terms.

We got him 30% below the rate we were quoted two years prior.

The conviction to walk away from the shoe store will also be fortified by the insight that time is a very powerful tool in negotiation. It is actually my favorite, because it is a naturally occurring process, nothing dirty to employ. In real estate it was a very revelatory asset. It peels away all the layers of bravado and stupidity and gets to the heart of the matter when you just sit on a deal and wait. If the other side is squirming, then it's working.

It's not a dirty trick—it's just water seeking out its level. If, in two or three years, the talent in any of my aforementioned examples is truly worth what their quote was, then they will be getting that figure from everyone and all projects will be making money, which justifies that rate. So in that case, time has proven the rate to be true, and they deserve that rate. But if that rate hasn't proven true, and they're wise, the fee will come down and they will be sitting across from me under the lights, ready to shoot something entertaining that illustrates their magnetic personality for all their future employers to see. I'm actually doing them a service. They should pay *me.*

There is one final situation in which walking away, and quickly, is preferred. It's not a matter of a shoe size, but rather a shoe-bomb. This is when, regardless of the deal you strike, either the talent or their representative are going to get in the way of your production. Regardless of whether or not you got a size 9, there's a time bomb sitting in the thing and it's going to blow your foot off.

After the first edition of *Missy Hyatt's Pajama Party* we actually tried to put some more editions of the show in the can. It was a gross deviation from brand, as we've already established, but for what it was—it worked. If the show had proven to be a hit, we probably would have kept going with it, and we are usually hesitant to cancel a series with less than three editions on the market anyway. Audiences could be slow to the concept, but it could gather steam. Perhaps the first guest on a series was the issue. If we have the resources, we could do a few and see what happens, but ultimately, whether or not we like it, the viewers are the final vote.

In keeping with that philosophy, we planned at least one more episode of *Missy Hyatt's Pajama Party*. So when I saw that lady wrestler Mickie James was doing the circuit, I reached out to the person handling her for an appearance in our area. I cannot remember the name of the man with whom I dealt, mainly because I never dealt with him again.

We thought she would be a good guest for the next edition of *Missy Hyatt's Pajama Party*. She was a decent size name at the time, had a fan following, and putting her with Missy might be fun. What the hell, let's give it a whirl. I still wasn't sure what this show was supposed to be. Mickie could have done a *YouShoot* of course, but I'm pretty cautious about booking women on that show. When a lady is sitting across from me, I can control the show. But *YouShoots* can be brutal with some of those fan questions and if I don't know that a lady can roll with that, then I don't want to take the chance.

Is this a double standard? Yup. Is it easier for me to ask Lanny Poffo about the size of Argentina Rocca's dick than it is to ask Maria Kanellis about the size of CM Punk's? Yup. Should it be? I don't know, but it is. Maybe it's because I have daughters.

Suffice it to say I knew I would have no problem with Tammy Sytch going along for the *YouShoot* ride, wherever that took us. Same goes for Missy Hyatt when she appeared on the show. Their reputations preceded them. I asked around about Amazing Kong and everyone said she was very cool and had a great sense of humor. They weren't wrong—she was one of my favorite *YouShoot* guests ever and the only guest to have me bend her over on the set.

Maria Kanellis was a bit of a question mark when we booked her. I didn't know her and didn't really get any feedback on her. Given that, I normally wouldn't have reached out but she was extremely marketable at the time. She'd just finished a stint on *The Celebrity Apprentice* on NBC and dated CM Punk, who was a WWE star at the time. So I made the call.

She was being brought in by a guy that we knew a little from the circuit. He was a cop up in Boston, a lieutenant no less, who did this talent booking on the side. At the time he had a big slate of lady wrestlers he was dealing with. Let's call him Kevin.

Our friend at Legends of the Ring, James Soubasis, vouched for Kevin and we booked Maria. Kevin proved to be a great agent and I always looked forward to booking through him. His deals were the quick handshake kind and he always delivered. His schedules stayed on track. He gave wrestlers the actual pitch from us, so there were never any surprises. I know for a fact that it was his selling that got guys like RVD, who didn't want any part of the shoot programming world, to agree to work with us.

But back then, for *YouShoot: Maria Kanellis,* we didn't know Kevin. I actually went to him through James so I didn't even talk with him. I just knew he was a serious guy, and was very protective of his lady wrestlers. He probably carried a gun.

On the prescribed date he delivered Maria to the suite, collected the money, and sat down behind the cameras to watch the shoot. He was pretty quiet and just looked on with his crazy cop-eyes. And there I sat—a laptop before me loaded with questions regarding CM Punk's dick, going lesbo with other girls, and a game called "Real or Fake." We leave very little to the imagination.

Throughout the show, as Maria giggled and cringed at what lay before her on the laptop screen, I kept looking over to Kevin who would lean forward when he didn't know what Maria was watching, craning his neck toward us, his eyes darting between Maria and me. What the hell was he thinking?

We took a ten-minute break in the shoot and Maria headed to the restroom. When she was out of sight, I looked over at Kevin. I couldn't pretend this show wasn't risqué at times, and Kevin piped up and said the first thing to me all day, in his thick Boston accent.

"She's hawt shit, ain't she?"

I breathed a sigh of relief. Yes, she was. She was laughing and having a great time and that was good enough for him. I think the gross-out factor is removed because guests eventually learn I'm a skilled host and though they might be talking about a wrestler's Johnson, it's all in good fun. There's no creep factor. Just a guess. Missy Hyatt had a much cooler observation when I mentioned to her how surprisingly chill Maria was.

"That's because I could tell she digged you." Great for the ego, though detached from reality. We won't address the grammar.

It came time to consider using Mickie James for our programming and I wasn't sure how *YouShoot* would go, so we thought it would be safer for her to do *Missy Hyatt's Pajama Party* with us for her first KC project. I reached out and texted the agent guy the details regarding our offer. This guy texted me back pretty quickly and it was clear I wasn't dealing with an Eric Simms or Kevin the Bad Lieutenant.

This mouth-breather texts me back in all caps, basically lambasting me for putting her on a pajama party show. He was rushing to the defense of the pinup girl he was undoubtedly whacking it to, and now fancied himself her representative. I'd hoped Mickie would have picked a virgin that could at least spell.

This guy was no doubt a friend of some guy who was promoting a show somewhere who decided to handle bringing in a pretty star of the ring so he could stare at her all day. It's sad but they're out there. These oafs are in the business to either ogle women or hang out with Mick Foley. Maybe some want to ogle Mick too.

I was sitting at a Japanese restaurant with my family and this became one of the unfortunate times some business related calamity arose and made me distant and short with them. Unless I handle the thing that is boring a hole in my stomach, I cannot rest. I told my wife I had to handle something and I called this dick. I politely tried to explain that he was unfamiliar with our programing and should reserve judgment until he knew with whom he was speaking.

"You said you want her to be in bed with pajamas," he began, "and I'm not gonna say that to her. She's a women's champion with a country album and—"

"I'll call you later." I hung up with the mark and went back to my sushi. I texted Anthony that this guy was offended and Mickie was probably a little prudish and we may want to reconsider. I put my phone away for the duration of the meal.

When I later decided I should get back to business, I awakened my phone and was met with a rather graphic porno picture in my texts.

"Her?" Anthony had texted, below an image of what appeared to be Mickie James shoving her spread vagina out of my screen. Couldn't say for sure, but it sure looked like her. A quick Internet search showed me that it was widely reported she was, in fact, an adult model for the fine publication *Leg Show*. How about that?

No judgment toward her, but imagine this shithead promoter going pious on me and talking to me like I was Larry fucking Flynt.

I sent him a text. With a photo.

"I apologize for not producing something more classy like this. I rescind my offer and will reach out when I decide to produce full-out porno. If you've spoken to Mickie already you can tell her your stupidity cost her a legitimate payday. Lose my number."

Walking away with such conviction, whether due to shoe size or shoe-bomb, requires you to frame the decision properly. If you're the type who will constantly question a decision and do the "what if" thing, then you'll need to work on losing that. If you frame it in the context of doing what's best for your feet, and accept that as an unwavering truth, you have the prerequisite skills.

14. Assessments

CONTENT IS KING, but data is your guide. You'll need that cold stuff to let you know if you're headed off the highway. Doesn't matter what you're driving if you run out of road.

Many times you'll be able to predict what most of your data will say. Because you're in the thick of your business every day, you'll know what's selling and what's having a harder time getting off the ground. For us, it comes as no surprise when we see our sales figures for a new Jim Cornette show. We know it's going to be a hit. Same for a show that stars Kevin Nash or, sorry guys, Vince Russo.

What was rather unpredictable for us was the incredible, early success of an investigative special we released called *Kevin Sullivan and the End of WCW*. The show was a real outlier and we contemplated the reasons for its success on dozens of occasions. The show is ten years old and I still don't know.

From a programming standpoint it had a lot of strikes against it. Firstly, it was not part of a branded series. When that special was released we had *Guest Booker, YouShoot,* and the short-lived series *My Side of the Story* up and running. As you know from being a viewer of your own favorite TV shows, you become invested in a series—the attitude, the writers, subject matter. You'll check out every episode. That's one of the things that building a series-based production company brought us—fan investment in our individual product lines.

But *Kevin Sullivan and the End of WCW* was not an episode of any of those. We'd only released one other investigative special, *Rebuilding the Sheik,* and it did slow sales. It wasn't a flop, but it was not expected to be a smash. It profiled Sheiky and his agent Eric Simms as they recounted Sheik's resurgence in popularity via his appearances on Howard Stern as well as viral videos of him going bonkers. Simms asked me about its sales almost weekly and beyond a couple of stoners who fell asleep on their keyboard and hit the "buy" button and Eric's mom, I think we sold some.

We'd just decided to film investigative specials—one-offs that are not part of a series and instead focus on a singular aspect of the wrestling business for each edition. We didn't expect a hit in that category—just a fun show about Sullivan booking as WCW faded.

I am a "Kevin Sullivan guy" for sure, but I didn't have unrealistic expectations regarding his drawing power. He'd launched the *Guest Booker* brand by being the inaugural guest on our first series. Come to think of it, he launched the damn company. But this was a weird format—a week-by-week analysis of the final months of WCW when Kevin was on the creative team. Kevin had been off TV for years and was not a shoot interview darling like Cornette.

Was it this inventive format—the week-by-week gimmick? Sullivan was quite entertaining and very much willing to tell tales out of school. That made for entertaining trailers. I was quite proud of my cover design, which then adorned all the web banner ads. It was very filmic, a dramatically lit close-up of Sullivan's face.

Was it all of that stuff together? Any of it alone? Who knows? My best guess is that it was a perfect storm of elements that resonated with viewers and then delivered on its promise, generating lots of word of mouth sales.

For whatever reason the show was working. The sales data on this show indicated something interesting. It wasn't explosive out of the gate, making us scramble to keep up with orders in its first weeks. It was more of a slow burn, selling steadily for *years* after its release. If we weren't as diligent with our data, poring over it all every quarter at our meetings, we wouldn't have noticed it was slowly accruing revenue quarter over quarter. It was becoming a top seller in our earliest years until we had bona fide smashes like *Guest Booker with Jim Cornette* that did numbers like we'd never expected.

The data didn't lie and it opened our eyes to elements we may have overlooked. It's no wonder we were so comfortable devoting an entire series to a week-by-week analysis of a federation when we launched *Timeline: The History of WWE* years later. Anthony always liked the concept of chronological exploration, and this show proved its value. When I had the idea for *Timeline* later, this format was a natural fit. It was the assessment of the data that lit the way, back in 2008.

One of the great things about small business in the modern age is the availability of very specified information. It's this information, the cold part of your business, that you will use to constantly monitor the health and well being of your company. And it's these tools and assessments that will indicate the more subtle need for adjustments. These indicators will guide your business by showing you the needs for change that The Blood does not see. The insight that your passion provides will not really help you much here. Fortunately, the cold part of business is learnable.

Our first big adjustment at KC was our transition from an mp3-based business to production of full-length videos. After we identified the need to change our entire product line, the line on which the company was originally founded (no small feat), we did have a distinct advantage. As participants and fans in the market, we were privy to the fact that a commitment to production values and unique formatting of subject matter would ensure differentiation. We knew we had to make the change, and The Blood told us how to change. We began producing shows we'd love to have seen, done the way we wished they had been done before.

We've had to make plenty of adjustments based solely on cold data, with no room for more divine guidance from The Blood. One of the earliest lessons we had to learn was about online shoppers' behavior.

There are several analytics websites that allow you to drop some html code on your website, and in return their service will feed you data on the behavior of those that visit your site. It's a remarkable study, and a real advantage to business owners. Imagine opening a brick and mortar store and having the ability to get a detailed report about which shelves shoppers spent the most time at. Or where they'd just come from. Or in which order they visit the individual displays and shelves. That data would be nearly impossible in a store. Online, it's as easy as a bunch of code and your investment of time studying the results. You can see what was clicked, in what order, and even how much time each surfer stayed on each page.

Studying that data was so revealing. A good analytics site will show you all of the above and so much more. You'll see what country your visitors were in, their operating system, and browser. Some of it may seem trivial but looking at the right data is crucial in maximizing the shopper's experience when visiting your site.

This is simply the online version of watching all of your shoppers navigate your store, which may be a commentary on how well or how poorly your displays are designed, and their location. Do you need to move those racks closer to the display window? Do it. Did your foot traffic increase? Digital translation: Move that link a little higher up on the page. Did the link get more hits? Ah, then it's better positioned now.

Online analytics will show you all that and more. I can unequivocally state that studying customer patterns and trends on our site was one of the most valuable contributions to our early success. Each site is different, so there's no way to learn this other than watching customers enter, browse, and exit your store, whether virtual or concrete. Is a part of your site or store hanging up your traffic? You're looking for obstacles to purchases, and you'll change them into paths to purchases. Get rid of obstacles.

If you're frustrating your customers because they can't find what they want easily, then you're doing everyone a disservice.

Analytics will tell you a lot about the navigation of your site. If a customer needs more than just a couple of clicks to find their item and its "buy" button, you have too many obstacles and distractions. Your more desirable items should be one click away from the customer's doorstep.

The Internet created Generation Now, whether you like it or not. The public wants their desires met instantly. So study those cold analytics and get it to them now. In studying the site data, you may initially be horrified to see how narrow your engagement time is with most of your customers. If you can keep someone on a particular page in your site for more than 5 seconds, you're doing remarkably well. What does that say about the importance of a well-streamlined site?

Assessments of your customer's profiles can be very helpful. A typical analytics service won't tell you the age range of your shoppers, or their gender. YouTube analytics do provide that, so if streaming videos are a big part of your business, then you'll be able see all that and more. But if you want to build an email list or just get general information about your fans, you'll have to go an extra step for that in the form of a survey of some kind.

It's a little more intrusive because it isn't transparent to your shoppers. I'm all about maximizing the shopping experience, and that includes speed, anonymity, and ease of use. If you hang someone up with a pop-up survey, I consider that to be risky to the process. Yet the information a customer can provide you in such a survey would be valuable to both you and them. You should work to find a way to make it as comfortable for the shopper as possible, yet still get enough data to validate the survey.

At KC, we waited until we were in business for a couple of years and had built a large and trustworthy fan base. We provided the customers on our opt-in email list a link to a short survey, I think it was five or six questions. We wanted to know ages, and some shopping preferences. They had the link in the same email newsletter that also provided all the usual new release information that we always included. When they had some time, if they wanted to answer the short survey, they could. It was simple and un-intrusive, sent to our reliable customers.

If your site is a registration-required site, you've already collected the customer's vitals, but their preferences and suggestions won't appear anywhere, so you'll still want to consider a survey geared toward those types of data.

The data that comes back will help you in product development and also in the design of your store, your site. If you're getting 75% of your traffic from males between 25-35, you'll want to change that pink splash page, killer. If that demographic is your target, then your marketing is spot-on. But your process needs some tweaking. Get some blacks and blues on that site. The aforementioned demographic is pretty close to a pro wrestling oriented site like ours, so we're right where we need to be. We're actually around 90% male. But if you sell a product for a mass audience, you'll definitely need to assess your marketing decisions if the demo that's being returned is that heavily young, male group. You've got to get some traffic from the opposite direction. Ask your wife why her friends would think your company sucks. Then make changes.

Your assessments will either confirm your decisions or indicate problems. They're the most honest indicator of your effectiveness so don't fiddle with the results. Let them be unabashedly brutal. In return, be equally vigilant about your corrective measures. Make the decisions that get you back "in the zone."

I created a tool at Kayfabe Commentaries that helps us stay in the zone. It's called the P-G-I Triad and it took four years of trial and error before it crystallized for me. I wrote about it and presented it at a quarterly meeting. It cited our company's successes and failures, all presented in terms of the triad. Sometimes my intensity and focus on these things gets a chuckle from the KC employees. I don't give as shit. You don't get anywhere by accident.

The P-G-I stands for profitability, growth, and innovation. These three components were the core of our early success. Your company may require a focus on different elements, that's up to you to identify. But for us, there's a test of profitability, growth, and innovation that our decisions must first pass. If I plugged one of our less successful projects into that triad, we'd immediately see which of these elements the show had failed, in retrospect. It's a decoder of sorts. Remember those old board games where a card with a printed answer was obscured by a jumble of red patterns and type? When you slid a transparent, red cellophane decoder over it, the red was cancelled out and you'd be able to see the answer. Our triad has a similar effect.

If I drop a less-successful show of ours into the P-G-I Triad, I might see that while the show contributed to the growth and innovation aspects of our goals, the show's exceedingly high production costs made for too difficult a breakeven point, so the profitability portion of the triad has been failed. It's called a "bad decision," in plain English.

If the biggest wrestling star in the world was available and willing to do a show with us, and we had developed the most ingenious concept ever, that would certainly satisfy the growth and innovation part of our P-G-I. But if we had to pay, say, $10 to this star for the interview, and based on our market experience we knew that we could expect to make only $9 or $10 in total sales for the resulting show, then this is usually a bad decision.

I say *usually* because, truth be told, there are sometimes ancillary reasons for green-lighting a bad decision, which would make it a far less bad decision. Could you consider the project a loss leader? Is the -10% sacrifice going to be a +25% gain in another way? Will that investment of 10% in the form of a loss on this project have intangible assets like heavy press coverage, exposure of your product line to new fans, or laying a foundation for future projects? Maybe it's something to consider then. But if this tanks in a big way, remember one thing—your P-G-I showed you the reality. You chose to ignore the warning and press on to pursue secondary gains, knowing short-term profitability was at stake. No "I told you so." It was a known risk.

Just as our P-G-I can assess individual products, it also serves as a credo on a larger scale, for our whole company philosophy. Our broad decisions should satisfy the P-G-I as well. Try it for your company—maybe this metric works for you. If you can say you're achieving consistent profitability, growth, and innovation in your industry, you're an undisputed success.

15. Collaboration

I'M A HUGE believer in the "sum of the parts" theory. The strengths of each gear in the machine compliment the function of another's. Your business is multifaceted and has very unique strengths and advantages. It may also have voids in certain areas. If used properly, your company's strengths can barter to fill the voids. A great way to do this is through collaboration with other companies.

At Kayfabe Commentaries I was always looking for good companies with whom we could do business. I'm also keenly aware of options we can add to maximize the experience at KC. The process is simply finding an element of our company that we can lend to another company, who will in turn lend us a strength of theirs. Those partnerships, if well thought out and designed cost-effectively, can be so valuable with minimal expenditure on either party's part.

Next time you are in a fast food burger joint, pay attention to the packaging of kid meals. There is a fine example of an exchange—the movie studio has a film for which they need to reach the children's audience. BugerPlace serves kiddie meals in specialized containers. In exchange for driving kids to the fast food place to get that cool new toy (there's some big bucks in that exchange too), the burger restaurant will further advertise the new film to the kiddie market by putting it all over the packaging of the kiddie meals, plastic cups, and also throwing in a .10 cent toy.

Be sure that you are aligning yourself with a company consistent with your brand. Your end result gain will actually be a long-term loss if your brand image is diluted.

Let's revisit our fisherman for a moment. His store will now be offering boating classes. As his students file in for class every Tuesday evening, Mr. Fisher will present a slideshow, videos, and some diagrams he made about fishing boats that are good for the local waters. It's an area of expertise for Mr. Fisher, so he can conduct an informative class. The pictures of the boats and the discussion will keep attendees engaged. He charges $25 for the four-week course that meets once a week for 2 hours each session. Ten die-hard fishing enthusiasts sign up to talk about boats and swap boating advice and anecdotes. Mr. Fisher will add $250 to his company's bottom line for sharing his time and knowledge.

Across town sits Billy's Big Ass Boats, a local company operating on the wharf. If Billy (of Billy's Big Ass Boats fame) were smart, he would have sought out Mr. Fisher when he first opened, and visa versa. If you're seeing a great opportunity for collaboration here, you're right on.

Billy can lease one of his boats out every Tuesday evening for four weeks. He'll even drive it while Fisher conducts the class at the back of the boat. Each week, Billy takes the class out on the waters on a different type of boat, each with different features and characteristics. Now, students not only get Fisher's knowledge and advice, they will get an on-the-water experience each and every week.

Applications for the "On the Waters" courses have now tripled. The die-hards are still there—those are the cats that would have paid to come and stare at slideshows of boats every week. But now Fisher has now managed to cross over into a new subset of patron. More casual fishing enthusiasts are now signing up to learn, and also have a good time getting out on the water since they don't often have the time to do so. Bring a beverage of choice, your rod, and have a fun class while the sun sets on the lake around you.

Of course the class now comes with much more value added so the cost is $100 to each student. Remember the attendance has tripled, so Mr. Fisher's revenue is now $3,000 for the four-week class.

Why on earth would Billy do this? What is he getting in return for taking his boats out every week? Every course Fisher runs will have 30 new faces meeting Billy, getting on his boats, signing up for his email list, and maybe even booking a spot on Billy's Saturday morning fishing charters he runs every week. Of course, each of the students in Fisher's class has been given a 20% off coupon for those Saturday fishing charters the moment they stepped on board for the class. As Mr. Fisher's class learns about boats, they are learning while riding on one of Billy's boats. They have to drive to Billy's Big Ass Boats on the wharf for each class. That kind of familiarity is priceless. It's truly a mutually beneficial arrangement. Especially when Billy asks for a 25% cut of class registration fees for the gains his boats have added to Fisher's course.

Several years before co-founding Kayfabe Commentaries I came across a website called The History of WWE (www.thehistoryofwwe.com). It's a fan site, with no official affiliation to the actual WWE, the world's largest and most famous wrestling federation. The site is a massive database of every live and televised wrestling event the site's owner could compile. You click on a year, a federation, and what you have is a list of every match of record, the city, and the fan attendance when available. It's quite a resource for the wrestling historian.

When we conceived our *Timeline: The History of WWE* series, I thought this site would be a great companion piece. Viewers of our series would love the detail contained in the site, and fans of that website would love to see it come to life with our interviews. There was clearly a marriage to be made here.

I reached out to Graham Cawthon, the site's owner, and pitched a joint venture wherein we would credit his website in each edition of our series, and also drop a link to his page on our sales pages on our website. In exchange, we would provide him a banner for each edition of our series, which he could strategically place on his website driving some traffic back to us.

In our example at KC as well as Fisher's store, each side benefited in strengthening their business and brand with little expenditure. I'm happy to steer our customers to www.thehistoryofwwe.com for additional information on the subjects covered in our *Timeline: The History of WWE* series. The site is thoroughly researched and takes great care to provide intricate details about pro wrestling's storied history. Graham Cawthon also created a Business of Blood with his website, so perhaps I also have a soft spot for it. His venture is a solo operation as far as I know and is an absolutely astounding amount of research and information.

Symbiotic partnerships can really fill out your product line and make for a more complete experience for your customers by adding new dimension. Everyone wins, so get in bed with someone. Just make sure your company's sensibility and brand is consistent with theirs.

At KC, the most common collaborations we enter into involve wrestling promotions. Someone running a wrestling show will usually put out some feelers as to who also might be interested in a particular talent on a particular date. If they can split the expenses several ways, while at the same time getting multiple paydays for the wrestler, then that works out for everyone.

Having said that, the wrestling underbelly is littered with humanity cast aside from traditional society. You have to proceed with caution and assume you'll be counting the honest denizens of that world on one hand. A few years back we entered into a working relationship with an independent wrestling federation called Pro Wrestling Syndicate, the company I mentioned earlier in the story about the man-ass that remained in the ring far too long for Kevin Sullivan's liking. The booker for PWS split from the company and his partner in the federation, and we ended up working with both of them separately, refusing to take a side. But that decision would soon be made for us.

I was dealing with new PWS owner Pat Buck who soon

rebranded the company as WrestlePro and kept running great shows, drawing great houses, and partnering with us for talent. His former booker, let's call him Pecker, started running a women's wrestling group and we partnered with him on using talent for our *Kayfabe Commentaries Bombshells* series. Pecker would consult with us on talent, we'd agree on which ladies to bring in, and they'd work in the ring for him and then for us on our new show. We booked four women as guests plus host Leva Bates. I worked out how much KC would be paying for each of them and they were all booked. Pecker sent me the invoices for all the expenses associated with the flights and hotels, and we were set. Pecker told me to just pay him in bulk and he'd pay the women their fees for both KC and his company.

"No, I hand my talent their money," I told him. "No offense, that's how we do business. That way, there are no misunderstandings." KC's money goes from my briefcase to the talent's hands for very good reason—transparency. Pecker went silent for a minute.

"Um, okay," he said.

I talked with Leva a couple of times before that weekend to go over the hosting duties and just the general format and direction of the show. We were all set, then I got a weird text from Leva.

Who is paying me for your show? she wrote.

We are. Why? I replied.

They told me that they would pay me for everything and I shouldn't go to you.

I knew what was happening. I'd put blinders on when I began reading about the rift between Pecker and Buck. When they split, I decided not to prejudge based on allegations in the wrestling media, preferring to reserve judgment if it ever became relevant in my business dealings with either. To that point, neither had shown me that they were less than trustworthy. But this was the first sign that something was amiss. Why was Leva being told I wasn't handling her money for the KC shows, when I'd been explicit about that with Pecker?

Because I was being robbed.

I asked Leva how much she was promised for both my program and the wrestling show. The figure she told me was less than half of what I was paying her alone.

She was being robbed. The minute I handed Pecker my envelope, there would have been a big hole in it. And I knew that meant all five women I booked through him were being robbed too.

I left my living room and told my oldest daughter to stay downstairs, daddy had to up and yell at someone on the phone. I haven't included a chapter in this book about the detrimental effects of owning a business on your family. I should have. Maybe it's exclusive to pro wrestling. Your business may require less aggravation.

After several tries I got Pecker on the phone and exploded. There was not even a 0 to 60—I left the garage doing 100.

"I'm the *one fucking guy* that kept doing business with you after you fucked over Pat—what a shithead I am!" I yelled. "You think you'd actually be able to rob me?"

This cocksucker actually began to defend his attempted theft by saying, "Well it's not my fault you are overpaying these girls. They shouldn't get half of what you offered them." That wasn't the point and it was none of his business what anyone was getting paid, just like it wasn't my business that he apparently paid these women like $50 for risking their damn lives in his ring. I was mad about everything.

"I am paying every one of those girls myself on Saturday and after that we are never doing business again. You and I are going to shake hands and play nice in front of everyone because I hate indie fucking drama, and I don't want to spook the guests. But when I walk out of there you are dead to me, scumbag."

On shoot day we loaded in and shot four segments of the show with Leva hosting Mia Yim, Santana Garrett, Kennadi Brink, and Kimber Lee. I paid the ladies myself and told them if anyone had anything whatsoever to say about paydays, they were to come right back to me. I didn't smear Pecker right then—I needed my shows and no drama. But now I hope they read this and know that they were about to be fucked out of 75% of their payday. I know Pecker is no longer in the business of promoting shows.

A year or so after this I did get a glorious opportunity to settle up with Pecker. He was doing a regular show with both men and women and had Scott Hall and Kevin Nash booked. They were doing a fan signing for him before the card began, and then Scott and Kevin were going to do an NWO-style promo in the ring to kick off the live event. Nash was in touch with me because he was coming to me to shoot an edition of *Guest Booker* after his in-ring segment for Pecker down in South Jersey at Starland Ballroom.

Nash was unhappy about the multiple people picking him up for each of the shots he had. He was doing his best diva act for me, and I played along, so sympathetic. Of course I wanted Nash to be happy, he was a major talent for us. But it also gave me an opportunity to go down to Peckermania and pick Nash up myself.

And I did. Just before his in-ring segment was to begin.

16. Diversify

LET'S SAY A stock investor is particularly excited about the prospects in the tech industry. He pours all of his investments into that market segment and holds a strong position in various tech companies, and maybe even a tech fund. A financial advisor would tell him that he's at great risk and should diversify. He'd be told to temper his risk by buying some bonds and spreading his investments across a few sectors. He needs to protect, or "hedge" in financial geek-speak, his investments. Why?

He should do this for the same reasons you will consider having multiple product lines or services in your business. Just focusing on one thing is a risk, even if you do that one thing really well. Your excellence in that field can actually work against you if you allow yourself to become too myopic. Even of you work tirelessly to perfect your core business or item, there are external swings and trends that can affect the life of your product. And if that's the only thing your company does, then it's affecting your business as a whole.

Stay away from market-based businesses or products. My old real estate friends will be annoyed by this, but I think deep down they'd agree. Don't anchor your efforts and innovation to the whims and miscalculations of the masses. Or in a worse case, to an entity like banks or Wall Street. No true-blooded entrepreneur would want their creation to be toppled by forces they cannot control. Anyone blessed with a strong entrepreneurial desire wants to be a decision maker. In a market-based business, that's the primary decision maker—the market.

In the first decade of the 2000s, the U.S. housing market was in the shitter. It sat decimated, having been plundered by poor decisions from buyers, poor decisions from their lenders, bad advice from mortgage gurus and appraisers, and widely varied competence of real estate agents and their brokers. From the top of that chain, the Federal Reserve, down through banks and mortgage brokers to the front lines occupied by agents, closing a deal was a house of cards back then.

Around every turn there was a bank reneging on a commitment, an appraiser pulling a bizarre number for the valuation of a property, a buyer lying on an application or doing something stupid with their money before closing, or an uneducated, desperate, ethically-devoid agent blowing up the deal.

Imagine tying your ingenuity and entrepreneurial skills to that crop? Your business would be in deep shit. It doesn't matter how great your real estate website or your FSBO (For Sale By Owner) tool is. Your success or failure is out of your hands. Don't fool yourself—you're not the boss in such an industry. I once told a real estate broker that the entire real estate business is a big restaurant. The kitchen is in the role of seller—they have a product that is either good or bad. The diner is buyer, looking at a menu and description, smelling the wafting gifts from the kitchen. The real estate agent is the waiter carrying crap back and forth and taking orders from the kitchen as well as the diner. And if either is displeased, forget about it. The broker is nothing more than the maitre 'd, poking around and hoping everything is going okay, making sure the silverware is clean and there's no one blocking the doorway. No one at the agent or broker level is in charge of a thing.

If you do decide to enter a market-based business and surrender your power to market conditions, then develop an alternative product line, like a great foreclosure advice seminar.

I won't belabor the point. Just stay away from businesses dramatically affected by markets. While true that almost every business is somewhat touched by surrounding markets, some industries are overloaded with such risk. Bear in mind that a great built-in hedge to market weather is your participation in a Business of Blood. People will only most reluctantly turn away from their passions and vices. I dare say that in even a poor market, people will turn to their passions for comfort. They may skimp on soap and hairspray, buying only the brands on sale, and they may not qualify for a mortgage; but they will certainly head out to fish on Saturday morning to return to that peaceful place in their soul that gets challenged by the events of the work week. As a company owner, you need to be their solace. Be that gift for them.

What do video game developers and casino operators have in common? Both of them are fun, and they do superb in good markets.

And guess how they all do in bad markets? Very well.

The common thread between them? The Blood. They both tap into customers' deep interests that are difficult to leave behind, even during a recession. That's not to say these businesses as a whole don't take a hit, but the declines (if any) are minimal compared to industry in general. Video games still moved $18.6 billion worth of product in 2009-10 (*The Street,* 1/14/11), which is a remarkable amount of money. True enough, that is a -6% drop from the prior year, but compare that to the computer software sector in general which saw a -13% drop, more than twice the damage. Why was *Call of Du*ty selling more than accounting software? The answer has nothing to do with quality or societal importance. It's all about the passion.

In Florida, one of the states hit most hard by the economic downturn in the late 2000s, saw its casinos jump *up* 10% in revenue in 2009 (*Miami Herald,* 3/2/11). With crippling unemployment and a skeletal housing market can this be true?

Sure. Casino games and gambling are a passion for many, a vice for some, and unfortunately an addiction for a few. Though we can debate the morality of the product, it's an illustration that passions will outperform necessities every time. Vices, innocuous or harmful, will be chosen over perfume. I pick on the health and beauty industry a lot. Nothing personal.

In all the above cases, we're talking about lifestyle-based businesses, heavily linked to the passions of their consumers. Think about your role as the owner of a Business of Blood—when things are good, you make your customers feel even better.

When it all goes to shit, you're the one place to which they can still turn for enjoyment. That's a nice place to be in the world.

A few months ago I was at our vendor table at the Legends of the Ring convention in New Jersey. I was signing copies of my books and talking about the hundreds of DVDs we had displayed for sale. I'm more than happy to make some time and chat with you if you've made time for our shows. Grab your cell phone so we can take a picture together.

Truth be told, I was feeling a little shitty that day. The shoot market is in the process of resetting and while fans of insider, wresting programming will always exist, the means by which they get their content is changing. The wrestling aftermarket is also getting sketchy. People are getting so much of what they want at home via the myriad outlets the Internet is now offering. We have several online delivery methods as well, with our OnDemand purchases, KC Downloadz, and now our own streaming subscription network called KC Vault.

That day at the convention I was looking around at vendors with small lines and in a near empty ballroom. Though our stuff can be purchased at home, many of those guys had wresters sitting at their tables that they'd brought out to sign autographs for fans. Many of those tables were merchandise dealers. Their business was suffering. *There is a market dying before me,* I thought.

While standing there longing for the good ol' days, I was pulled out of that malaise by two fans who approached me, only about fifteen minutes apart. The first shook my hand and I prepared to hear how he loved The Ho-Bag or What a Dick segments of *YouShoot.* Instead, he looked me in the eyes and told me about being laid up after a serious surgery on his jaw. It was excruciating and he couldn't really talk or eat for a month, and we'd helped him get through it with our shows. He said he watched a ton of our programming and it kept him going through the pain and the depression that was setting in.

Not long after that encounter, another guy came up and told me about a leg injury he'd sustained which laid him up for weeks. Our entire *Timeline* series was his sunshine during the cloudiest days of his life. I've had literally dozens of these encounters and still more on email. It's always a life affirming moment for me when someone comes up to me in person. They look me in the eyes as they thank me and remind me that my work with KC is more than just entertainment.

Sometimes I forget. Sometimes I need to be reminded.

That stuff touches my soul and it goes beyond the discussion of market and The Blood, but it should serve as a lesson there as well—people with whom you share The Blood do not place your brand of product or service in the same neutral category as their brand of soap and hairspray. Okay, I said I wasn't doing that anymore…as their socks and underwear.

In our case, I've always said that content is king. Millenials will laugh at that old-timer's credo, instead suggesting we should be trying to innovate some technology or distribution platform we could sell. But if you own the best shows out there, they will eventually play on every new platform that is to be created. You'll be a part of every new media technology to come. They'll all need you.

This market shift in content delivery is in no way making our programming less important. We are still the best shoot producers in the world and the litany of WWE-produced content only confirms that. Our honesty and grittiness can never be replicated by the shareholder-owned company. The challenge is in the pricing model, and unfortunately that's a reality we're attacking now.

But even after all this risk-aversion you've employed by staying out of a market-based business and being a slave to uncontrollable elements, you'll still need to insulate yourself from being cast into oblivion. The market may not be the demon here, but rather it's likely to be a competitor, technology, or a trend. Point is, if you have other revenue streams you're not sunk altogether if a segment of your business becomes challenged. Stay ahead of the curve by consistently emphasizing innovation and you'll always be firing your musket first, rather than being fired upon.

There's an art to developing ancillary revenue streams without over-saturating your brand, which will do long-term damage. Here's yet another instance where Businesses of Blood have a decided advantage over cold businesses. You'll likely know instinctively whether or not your proposed product lines are consistent with your brand image, thereby being true brand extensions, rather than just more stuff. Your gut will tell you.

17. Know Your Market, Part II: Know It Like A Scientist

KNOWING YOUR MARKET as intimately as you know a loved one assumes a very emotional and passionate bond, and knee-jerk decisions about your Business of Blood will come from that place. But it's also necessary to know your market from the cold place as well. It's a little like performing surgery on that loved one. There must be a clinical side of you that can process market information and put informed decisions into action from there.

We all know bad business decisions are usually caused by a lack of the scientific insight. I can say personally, that there have been

KC releases that were given a much longer road to profitability than needed. The reason for that was a lapse in market judgment. We know the market intimately and were personally excited about projects while we ignored that project's likely sales. If you are running a lemonade stand and you've decided that you absolutely love tomatoes, therefore you will be adding tomato juice to your lemonade, you'd better be certain your customers will pay for tomato lemonade juice. This example seems silly, but in some cases that's exactly what one may be tempted to do when possessed by, and therefore distracted by, personal tastes beyond what their market will accept.

You or someone in your company should have a good sense of what the market is for a particular venture. Since this is a Business of Blood that you're intensely passionate about, you already know what would be interesting in your universe of buyers. But there's a cost to the production of any product and you need to predict the approximate return you will get on the investment.

There are few ways to do this. Once you've been in business for a while, you'll become familiar with the return of certain products and the expected return of similar products. Anthony and I communicate that way all the time when considering shows for production. I'll get a call offering us Brodus Clay and I'll reach out to Anthony.

"They want $5 for Monster BC," I'll ask. "Where do you think a *YouShoot's* sales would land?"

"Not much more than Matt Sydal's."

In our *Timelines,* our 90s editions are the most popular across both WWE and WCW brands. The years of the ratings wars were hot, and those episodes do very well. If you can add a high profile guest like Eric Bischoff or Kevin Nash, it brings that episode to the next level. It's 4-figure sales versus 5-figure sales, and knowing those baselines lets us make prudent decisions.

Though you may feel the market would like or need something, you may further discover that no one will pay for it in the numbers that justify its production. There's a hard reality to business—if you're not profitable, you'll be gone. Don't buy into the pervasive notion created by the Internet generation that everything should be free. You can definitely add value to your products and offer extras, and I would implore you to do so. But if your venture doesn't make any money you can't make more product. And you're done.

Nothing is free, let's get that out of the way. Any company that stays in existence is getting their money somehow. Yes, the download of that song may be only $1.29 or maybe even free if you illegally downloaded it from a file share service. But the premium will be built into the price of the concert ticket when you go see that artist. There is a reason a concert ticket starts at $99. You may think it's wonderful that you can stream 200 movies a month for only $9.99, but when you do eventually go to a movie the tickets will soon be twice the price. Either that or you'll be staring at advertisements for a fair portion of your time in the movie theater.

Successful media companies are getting adept at making up for the losses that digital piracy and devaluation are causing. You're paying somewhere, either with money or time. Many people don't realize this. Personally I'd rather go back to the time when I had to buy CDs for $15, but a concert ticket was $30. Or when there were no commercials in the movie theater, except for a few trailers. I don't know about you but I'm sitting through more and more ads on the Internet now too. But this is where we are. And it's your responsibility as a company owner to find ways to make up the losses that the digital revolution is creating. We are trying. But more on that in Part Four.

Perspective is important in considering this digital revolution. Though it does challenge content producers' profits, it also gives us wonderful gifts that were previously impossible to obtain. The digital age has closed the chasm between product and customer, allowing for easy access—anytime, anyplace. Consider that there was a time where a company's touch with the customer occurred only when the customer saw an ad, or saw the actual product on the shelf.

Today the Internet gives you a ton of potential points of contact with consumers. You have direct access to them via e-mail, Facebook, Instagram, Twitter, and they you. Many of the newer Businesses of Blood that exist today are made possible because of the digital revolution in the first place. Recording one's own music and distributing it oneself would have been previously impossible, or at least very, very cost prohibitive. My mother can buy a USB microphone and start a podcast today. The opportunities created by the digital age need to be considered alongside the detriments of those advances and the devaluation of intellectual property. What giveth life also taketh away.

Back to scientific market knowledge. You need to develop that split personality—to be both a passionate participant in your market, yet still objectively assess the viability of a desire that exists in that market through cold calculation. As mentioned before, your gut will not help you here. This half of your total market knowledge comes from information and data, either intrinsically learned or researched.

In our specific market there is an expected range of sales for programs that deal with a particular era in pro wrestling. Old school, nostalgia programming, while fascinating and historically needed, appeals to a smaller market segment than does slightly more current era wrestling subject matter. Even the shift from a show that deals with 1985 to a show that deals with 1995 would likely mean a 20% increase in revenue right off the bat, regardless of the guest. That data runs counter to my own personal Blood, but that doesn't matter much. The Attitude Era outsells the Hogan Era in shoots. And if the shows are salacious and controversial in nature, that means even more sales.

How did we get this market knowledge? Firstly, by selling plenty of both so we had information to study. Then once we had the cold stuff to dig into, we did. Our marketing and budget decisions are based on both. A popular wrestler from the 70s and 80s may feel they should be paid X amount of money for a show because they are "worth that" and in their hearts, my heart, and the hearts of the fans, they may be worth that and even more. But the only thing that truly determines their worth is the return that their show will yield. Unfortunately their heart, my heart, and the fans' hearts don't know that value. But my head does, and it's my duty to break off negotiations and move on if their financial expectations differ from the reality I know to be true.

Another tendency to avoid, which is caused by The Blood, is our errantly sticking with a project for too long despite mounting evidence that you should bail out. We always know when a project is in trouble, but sometimes we add confusion by having an unhealthy commitment to it. It's no different from staying with an unfaithful lover after the point of no return, or working feverishly to save a precious, but sinking vessel. Your scientific market knowledge should overrule your passionate market knowledge and signal when it's time to pull the plug.

Here are all the series we've had to cancel in our first 12 years:

1. *Ringside.* This was the first to bite the dust. We launched this in 2008 shortly after the success of *Guest Booker* and *YouShoot,* which were our first two out of the gate. The show was an attempt to capitalize on the mp3 audio commentary tracks we launched our company with, wherein a wrestling star walked you through their matches and feuds of note. The big problem here was that we couldn't show the match footage, as we didn't own any of it.

We built the set to resemble a ringside table from the 70s and 80s, complete with the boxy monitor and colorful, foam microphone covers. The guest sat beside me and watched the matches on the monitor that faced away from the camera, and we discussed what was going on, who the opponent was, the venue, and everything related to the match on the screen.

You see the problem there, right? A monitor facing *away* from the audience. It was flawed in concept.

We shot three editions with guests Vader, Demolition, and Terry Funk. All three had very interesting matches and feuds to discuss, but that wasn't the issue. Maybe it was the host—me. After two releases we decided to hire journalist Bill Apter to take over the hosting and we renamed the show *Bill Apter at Ringside.* Well, it didn't mater if we put Apter at Ringside or on Mars—sales stayed down.

2. *My Side of the Story.* I loved this one. We brought in two guys that had a famous feud and interviewed them separately, asking each the same questions, then brought them together at the end for a discussion about what each had talked about. We included a handbook with the first edition, outlining every detail about their

feud you could ever want to know. We even had a comprehensive list of every match Greg Valentine and Tito Santana ever had with each other. It was brilliant and we did two editions—Tito and Greg, then Nikita Koloff and Magnum TA.

There were two problems here. Firstly it was double the cost of any other show because we needed two stars for each episode, including all their travel and associated costs. Scheduling was challenging too, as they often had separate obligations even while in the same town and we needed significant time to shoot each guy separately, then bring them together. We couldn't book another show for that same day.

The other issue was the format. Fans had only seen linear discussions in shoot interviews. This was pretty cutty and it was all history and no road and rat stories. It appealed to that more narrow historian-fan, and coupled with the increased expenses it couldn't make the money that justified its existence.

3. Missy Hyatt's Pajama Party. Can you even call one edition of something a "series?"

4. Ring Roasts. This was less a series than recorded live events, but we still had to make the decision to pull the plug on the live aspect as well as the video releases. The first edition with The Iron Sheik was most consistent in concept because he was on the road doing comedy with a group called The Killers of Comedy from the Howard Stern Show. Plus, Sheiky was a shoot interview favorite. Sales were good but the expense of the massive live show created a large hurdle to clear. I could have had a higher profit margin by just sitting down with Sheiky alone.

Then for *Ring Roasts 2* we brought in Terry Funk as the guest of honor—one of the most beloved men in the wrestling business. People got up and blew him instead of roasting him.

For *Ring Roasts III* we brought in the ringer—Jim Cornette. This would be the litmus test for the *Ring Roasts* concept. Everything that Jim touched in our catalogue turned to gold.

Except *Ring Roasts III.* Wrestling fans like comedy, and they like wrestling. They don't like comedy about wrestling. Lesson learned, series cancelled.

5. Wrestling's Most. Another one of my favorites goes belly-up. This was a countdown show that resembled the VH1 countdown shows that were pretty popular at the time, wherein a dozen or so wrestlers count down your votes for a wrestling topic, like *Wrestling's Most Controversial Moment* or *Wrestling's Most Effective Heel.* It was so much fun to shoot and edit, and hearing the stars comment on where the fans placed their votes was once again connecting fans directly to our programming.

I don't know why it didn't resonate with fans but the series couldn't gain traction and we released like 8 of them. This is right when online posting and piracy began to swell and bite into our sales of shows, so unless your numbers were quite big and could mitigate the effects, your sales would be hurt.

6. Raven's Restler Rescue. This was a reality makeover show wherein ECW star Raven would take a young, independent wrestler, rework their character, and then send them into the ring to see if the new gimmick would go over with fans. This was our attempt at the shoot interview 2.0. We were sensing the market was tiring of the traditional shoot due to time and an infestation of podcasts telling hours of stories for free.

Programming like *Raven's Restler Rescue,* if it succeeded, could have lit the way for the next revolution, whereby stars of yesterday could again command decent fees. Shoot producers like us could begin crafting unique, reality programming with the stars, putting them in entertaining situations that spotlit their knowledge and charisma. If they were telling their road stories for free on a podcast, they could at least be paid to makeover a wrestler's character on video. It would put emphasis back on production and differentiate itself from storytelling into a USB microphone.

Raven's Restler Rescue didn't get footing. As of its release, the shoot market had become so decimated that I'm not sure anything would have gotten footing. But we weren't wrong for trying this. We identified the changing market and knew that shoot programming would need to change as well. Raven was great and the shows were funny. It was at this time we started to suspect that *any* ala carte programming wouldn't fly in this new market where Netflix-style subscriptions are the norm. This might've been a great subscription network show, wherein each individual show doesn't have to hold its own weight so much as become part of a great ensemble of shows. But we didn't yet have our own subscription network, so *RRR* was put to bed.

7. *Bombshells.* This was always a tough one in my mind. We'd had a business relationship with a ladies wrestling organization so we had access to a talent pool of the finest in independent women's wrestling. We didn't have any programming that specifically and exclusively addressed that market segment, so there were signs that this show could do something. We found a great host in Leva Bates and booked some great guests for the first string of shows.

But there was something that was always troubling me—data. Some time before doing *Bombshells,* World Wrestling Network, our OnDemand vendor, sent me pie graphs of program hours streamed on WWN to justify yet a third increase in bandwidth charges to us. The illustration of their point illuminated something about ladies' wrestling programming. WWN was showing us that KC was generating about 85% of the traffic on their network, with Evolve and ladies' feds Shimmer and Shine accounting for the remaining 15%, and Evolve was the great majority of that. People just didn't pay for indie women's wrestling. That was more than confirmed with the butyrate of our *Bombshells* releases, and we put in overtime trying to pump up excitement for the series.

8. Gabe Sapolsky's Next Evolution. This was an attempt to spotlight the contemporary independent stars before they headed for WWE's NXT, for which Gabe's Evolve fedeation was functioning as a feed in. We got the tip about who was getting called up, and we brought them in to do an edition of *Next Evolution.* It was a great concept and a system that really worked.

We had great talent for the first three shows in Rodereick Strong, Chris Hero, and Johnny Gargano, and they sat with Gabe and went over their best matches from Evolve. This time we could actually show the matches, unlike the ill-fated *Ringside* series. Gabe owned Evolve and granted us full rights to the matches, along with WWN, the distributor. We put a ton of advertising and press behind this launch. It never took off and saw the customary three editions before termination.

I really think that our last three cancelled series launches fell victim to that market shift away from per-program purchases. These three shows should have a place in the shoot programing landscape and I think some of these shows could find a home in our network system.

We produce 9 series that have survived the axe and are part of the ongoing programming plans for KC. That's not a bad ratio for a production company. It's all about finding the right idea and finding out if the data correlates to your vision.

Remember you do have a safety net, and that is The Blood. Your misses will never sink to drastic depths because The Blood has ensured your product will be somewhat engaging. The New Coke debacle of 1985 would never have happened if a truly passionate fan ran their company. Changing the taste of something so iconic and identifiable as Coca-Cola would have been unthinkable to a Coke mark. They may have considered a drastic rebranding or repackaging, but changing the taste would never have been on the table.

One of our attempts at diversity during our fat years was Heat-Wear, a T-shirt line based on our programming. Shows are a hit, so shirts about those shows will also be a hit. Right?

Wrong. It wasn't a total miscalculation. The shirts were thematically aligned to our programing and the sensibility of the shows. We were okay with branding. But we did nothing special in getting them out. We just designed the shirts, designed a correlating website, and did some advertising on our KC site. We added a buy button below the shows also. But as always, the market sits as judge and jury and the verdict was "move on." We still have some Heat-Wear if you like to collect relics.

Your passion for your Business of Blood should work to keep it out of harm's way. It's an instinct not unlike a parent's. A child is usually never safer than under the watch of a caring parent. You may make a bad decision here or there but it will likely not be on a scale causing massive damage. The trick to keeping the child or the business safe is flipping your mindset from emotional to analytical. You love to see that big smile on your happy child, but letting them open that third candy bar will land them at the dentist for an unhappy session.

18. Adjustments

LET'S CONSIDER THE following metaphor—big business as a gigantic ocean liner cruise ship. I'm a visual person. If you ask me what time it is I'll grab a pad and draw you a watch. Just bear with me. You don't have to go far.

Inside of our massive cruise ship are hundreds of crew members, all with individual jobs to do, but they all contribute to making the ship run smoothly. Someone is steering, people are cooking, many are serving, some are entertaining, but all are making the machine function.

Let's add our Business of Blood to the marketplace, or in this example, the open seas. We're a speedboat. We just have a couple of people with us. You can drive the speedboat. I'll stand here and help out.

How do you think each boat will respond to turbulence? The big ship will get bounced around a lot less in choppy waters. Its structure is such that it can withstand battering. Our small speedboat could be in real danger if the waters get too rocky. We're not built to withstand a great amount of punishing weather. If it's bad enough it could mean the end of us. The big ship can plow through the temporary wrath of the storm. We need to do some real quick thinking.

Fortunately for us, we have some advantages before we ever hit the eye of the storm. Technology is such that us little guys can have access to the same information about the waters that the other big ships also have. That information, along with some foresight, can tell us some trouble may lie ahead. Even if we don't have much time, we can make some adjustments.

If both ships needed to steer out of the way of danger, which ship would make the quicker adjustment? And which would be able to get their crew reassigned and working toward a new direction faster?

Exactly.

Our small boat is more nimble than the massive operation that is the ocean liner. Our rapid adjustments can keep us out of harm's way so we never have to find the eye of the storm. It's up to us to steer that boat properly and holler over our shoulder, "Hang on, we're turning east." That big cruise ship has a lot more going on. Add some confusion to the mix and try and swing that bad boy around quickly. It'll take miles to make the turn. We're already headed in the other direction.

Adjustments in big business happen slowly. There's a chain of command a million miles long and that's filled with a lot of egos with opinions. They're all gonna weigh in with their suggestions. All departments will be consulted. Their product lines are in varying states of the supply chain, from factory to the warehouse, to the shelves. The company's advertising is set, ads currently bought, and more in production for next quarter. A small change can be a headache. A big one could upset the applecart.

It's up to a Business of Blood to use that nimble quality to its advantage. The Blood gives us a great advantage in the way of market knowledge and insight. That will certainly help hone our sonar and allow us a peek at what coming.

But you'll need to be aware of the cold part of your business also. Those numbers will also indicate a problem. Keep checking the health of both your company and your product lines. Then make changes. That's steering out of the storm.

At Kayfabe Commentaries we are now in the process of a big market adjustment as we look at moving our programing to an entirely subscription-based network format. Prior to this, our biggest market adjustment came about 6 months into our existence. Our original business was recording downloadable mp3 audio files of wrestlers doing commentary tracks for their historic matches. It was an idea that had never been brought to the industry. We employed our idea, born on Blood, and put to use some cutting edge technology that allowed us to sell downloads online.

We'd bring a wrestler in, have them watch 8 or 10 of their most historic matches, and in real-time they'd get on headset with me and discuss the intricate, inside details of what we were seeing. It was akin to the director of a film recording their commentary track for a DVD. iPods were all the rage and now you could go to our site to download the tracks, put them on your device, and watch your DVD of the match while listening to the track and experience the historic matches in a brand new way.

This was a unique product and on paper it was a model that seemed foolproof…until our cold data told us otherwise.

They sold at a modest pace. We began to get some coverage in the wrestling media and everyone thought it was a cool idea. What we didn't know was that our market demands far less work on the part of the customer. Firstly, we were asking them to download the file. A large segment of our fan base was the fan of classic wrestling. The age bracket of a fair portion of them was older and many had insufficient computer speed in 2007 (and some today as well). The downloading aspect was a problem.

Then we had the issue of their having to move the file to portable media. Some of the more tech-savvy had no problem with this. But still another portion of our market would have great difficulty. Then we required them to have a video copy of the match accessible somewhere. Remember, we were selling the audio, but we didn't own the rights to any of the matches. The fan was on their own, as far as the visual element was concerned.

Further, they'd have to start the audio and the video at a designated point so their experience would be in sync while they watched and listened. If the phone rang and they had to pause and restart all the media to stay in sync they'd have further stress added. It was a great idea but it posed too many challenges.

We knew we could provide the same kind of insider information and the same fan experience if we moved to video. The shoot DVD market was a competitive one. There were a few long-time players in there from whom we'd have to win market share. But we already knew there were lots of customers available to convert. We knew this because Anthony and I were two of them. As viewers of these shoot DVDs, we knew what that market lacked. We watched them back when they were often traded with others online, on VHS tapes, and not much had changed in those productions other than the media. We knew we could make a big splash by being very different.

We had had to create a customer base with our initial mp3 commentaries. Nothing like that existed. Like the speedboat, we flipped a switch, changed our entire focus, developed *Guest Booker,* and got into the business of converting customers in the shoot interview market. From a traditional business sense, it was a radical change. The product line changed and we went from a space that we had basically invented, to a new, existing market segment of video production and distribution. The written business plan (if we had ever bothered to do one) would in essence have been torn up and written anew.

But we were a Business of Blood. We were two fans with a small business, intense market knowledge, great instincts, and nothing to lose. Making that change was as easy as calling Kevin Sullivan's agent and booking him for an edition of a high-concept shoot program we had come up with called *Guest Booker*. I had already spent many years in entertainment from the production end and the performance end, and Anthony had his time split between production and computers. We were naturals at what we were setting out to do, in addition to being consumers—from rock fans to rock stars. We knew we'd pull it off.

We were able to transition into that new market by seeing the waters were problematic, and swinging the boat around quickly.

Part Three:

Growing It

19. Targets and Goals

YOU DON'T GET somewhere by accident. Both failure and success have a road paved with decisions that lie before them. Some decisions prove to be good ones, some less so. They usually lead to a predictable destination based on which set of choices you act upon.

A Business of Blood's early stages are loaded with start-up tasks to keep you scrambling to gain footing. You'll be busy studying the analytics, developing products and ideas, and trying to get noticed by customers and industry. It's quite easy to forget about looking down the road and planning for the future. You should be constructing a mental picture of where you'd like to go, both from a company as well as a product standpoint. Your goals will require you to chart the course to get your company to where you envision it. Your targets, however, will be the rungs on the ladder you're climbing. Your targets are the stepping-stones to your goals. In short, goals are your bigger picture; targets are your more immediate achievements.

Targets are usually associated with cold data. Targets can be revenue, net profit, a margin, a customer base, a number of subscribers, a customer approval rating, whatever. It's a specific number you're trying to hit, in a designated period of time. Once your Business of Blood is up and running you'll see what targets are realistic for your company. You have to be faithful to those targets; therefore they need to be realistic. There's no point challenging yourself and your workers to hit an unreasonable number. Strive for realistic growth. 10-15% annual growth in revenue and cash flow is a very respectable number.

Both of those should be emphasized. Too often, pursuit of revenue sacrifices the bottom line. The big dogs are guilty of that too. Desperate for that quarterly number, companies will eye the revenue only. If you're not carrying money down to the cash flow line, not much else will matter in short time. It may seem like Business 101, but take a second and go on the Internet and checkout Yahoo Finance or MSN Money. I want you to see how often companies of every size lose sight of that basic tenet. Select a company and look at their revenue growth every year on a 10-year statement. Then check their cash flow statement. Do they correlate? If they're growing revenue at 10%, are they also growing cash at a comparable rate? Check a few companies and it won't take you long to discover that most companies fail this test. Revenue is what you make; cash flow is what you keep. Too often they're not balanced.

The reasons for this are many. But the basic info is all you need to know—somehow, someway, that business is spending beyond its means. The cost for that revenue growth is too high and unless it's a capital investment that will pay dividends down the road, it's a recipe for bankruptcy.

There are instances where that is necessary, or at least unavoidable. Occasionally a large lawsuit must be settled or a penalty is paid. Maybe the company's expansion into Bolivia required the construction of a new plant in South America. In such a case that large expenditure is considered a *one-time expense* and its deleterious effect on the bottom line for that year isn't necessarily a sign of mismanagement. (Assuming we're ignoring the grounds for that lawsuit.)

Another large one-time expense is often a technology overhaul. A company may explain a weak bottom line by saying, "We used our cash investing in better, newer, more efficient equipment." In your early stages, you'll likely be reinvesting revenue into your company, and you should. It's a great investment, provided that money is making some aspect of production easier. It isn't all about money on the surface. If that new machine frees up some of your time then that's also valuable. You now have more time to go design the website, meet vendors, make calls, do interviews, conceive that new product, etc.

The flaw here would be filing technology as a one-time expense in your mind. Be sure to allot a part of your budget to technology every year. Year One, your computer may be your only large tech expense. Year Two you may need two or three pricey software programs. Year Three you may add a laptop to your arsenal. By Year Four, it may be time to replace that desktop PC you started on. Are these really one-time expenses? Technically yes, on the spreadsheet, as you're not repeatedly incurring them as you would postage, rent, salaries, insurance, and the like. But don't look at technology as anything less than a repeated investment in your growth.

At the level that our Business of Blood operates, assuming we're not yet raking in millions in revenue, it's easy to see where our expenses inflated and deflated cash flow. As a start-up, some or all of your first three years will likely show a loss in your net cash. Putting the pieces in place can be costly up-front in relation to how much revenue you'll be generating right out of the gate. Your start-up capital should be working to cover the expenses that your sales aren't. But that start-up capital has to end and your business must become self-sustaining. That's actually the very definition of a successful business—one that operates off of the cash it generates, and retains some in the end.

You'll get there by setting realistic targets and goals. Those targets need to have means by which to achieve them. Simply saying, "We want 15% growth in revenue and 10% growth in net cash flow" is great. That's the target I usually set at KC. But with that target comes a mountain of strategies needed to get there. You have to announce where you want to go, but also how to get there. Without means, your targets are just prayers. I don't know how many deities there are out there to which I can pray, but none I've ever heard of work in my industry. So it's up to the strategies that Anthony and I conjure up to make it happen.

20. Meetings

DISCUSSIONS OF TARGETS and goals should be happening at your meetings. They're very important and you need to schedule them if you have partners or employees. In this day of text and email, it's easy to fall into the trap of minimal interaction, and for basic day-to-day stuff that's fine (and often preferred). But you also need time with all involved parties in the room. Brainstorm, plan, whatever. If you're solo in your venture, take periodic, one-hour planning sessions. No busy work, though—think, doodle, scribble, have a cigar.

The meetings can be as formal or as informal as meets your needs, but give your business the respect of at least a few meetings per year. Actually, if you incorporate (and you should), you'll need to have at least one mandatory meeting per year, with recorded minutes. I think it's healthy to plan on quarterly meetings. It's easier to string your results together over four quarters to arrive at the desired final score—that being your annual targets.

At KC we always had four quarterly meetings and one annual planning meeting. The quarterly meetings were structured around the cold targets, for the most part. They reviewed the financials of the previous quarter, then forward looking initiatives for company, marketing, and production.

Our annual planning meeting is driven by broader topics. In them, we are more focused on the goals and direction of Kayfabe Commentaries for the next 12 months. Companies are dynamic, changing, growing things. You have to monitor, assess, and plan. Set your targets and make a plan to get there, and then review why you did or didn't make it.

Our friendly fisherman's store is doing quite well. Within his first year he paid off any startup debt, and finished the year with a small profit after all expenses and salaries. His business can be considered a success. Now it's time to focus on growth.

Based on his market, his annual financials, and his business' needs, Mr. Fisher decides that a 10% growth in sales would be an attainable target. He also thinks that the storeroom is getting a bit crowded with all the supplies and merchandise. If his business is to grow and hit that 10%, he'll need to add even more stock obviously, crowding that back room even further. He needs space. There's an expense in the near future, it is clear.

Mr. Fisher's goals for the coming year are to build an extension to his rear storeroom. He also plans on launching a personal instruction course, wherein he teaches a small group of paying students how to use the right lures, the right rods, and general techniques for a more successful fishing excursion.

There's a symbiotic relationship between Fisher's goals and his targets. His company's goals will help make those targets attainable. With the larger stockroom he can now handle more product, which can be more widely advertised along with the new classes, which will all add revenue. That revenue will first fill the gap for what's been spent on expansion, and then beyond that Fisher will focus on continuing to bring that added revenue to the bottom line. Don't forget that all-important relationship between revenue and cash flow. Make it your mantra.

If you're doing it right, sales should yield more sales. Fisher's got a good system in place by adding his classes. The students finish the class right there in the store, among all the merchandise they need to buy in order to fish. Not a bad plan.

Fisher will check his numbers on a quarterly basis and ensure that his goals are being met and initiatives are succeeding. The important thing to note is that each step in the process and the associated cost is justified by growth. If he threw all his money at the stockroom extension and new products right away, his well may have run dry. But by waiting for successes to justify playing his next hand, his targets and goals act like steppingstones to achievement.

21. Bottom-Up Marketing

"DON'T TRUST ANYONE over 30." That was a popular credo of the 1960s in America as the post-30 crowd was seen as conformist and part of the establishment. They weren't part of the enlightened group, or so it was believed by the under-30 crowd, who were fostering social change.

Today that type of sentiment of distrust is very much alive in advertising. The trust factor between a company and a consumer is greatly fragmented and it's totally understandable. After decades of buying the great, new car, we watch the model's brakes fail, cause dozens of crashes, and then learn that the company was aware of the defect. They didn't tell me that when they crawled through my television and into my living room. All they said was it was a great, new car.

We watched toy companies allow their products to be so poorly and cheaply manufactured overseas in China with so little oversight, that they contained toxic levels of lead. Then they made cute commercials, crawled through our televisions and into our living rooms, and spoke to our children. Our kids saw the colorful commercials and were told the toys were fun.

Our televisions are loaded with goofy infomercials hawking the latest gizmo that will surely change our lives for the better. You can tell just by watching that the results are being staged and simulated, and we're told so in tiny, unreadable type at the bottom of the screen that reads something like "You are watching a dramatization…results may vary." If you ask me, I think that should be in giant font, splashed across the screen because it's an admission that everything we're seeing is fake! It's deception. So much of advertising still is.

The really funny thing about this deception is that we always know it. Do we really believe that this glob of goo that is squeezed onto a rag will really erase a 10-inch gouge on the hood of a car? Even if we buy the product, we do so with a healthy dose of skepticism. We're accustomed to being lied to by the sales business. We know all salespeople are full of shit 90% of the time. Truth of the matter is, when an outstanding product is discovered by the masses, word of mouth does most of the selling. And it certainly does the best selling of all. Customers become the proverbial evangelists and tout the product or service's merits to friends and colleagues. This is a million times more valuable than any ad or demonstration. Why?

The answer is trust. Your friend or co-worker has already passed the tests that allow them to be ingratiated into your life.

Their word is respected and reliable, with no agenda. This marketing carries a ton of weight. An amalgamation of this is what is considered *bottom-up* marketing. It cannot be manufactured, and it must be genuine to really work. It's more than just testimonials, which are usually staged and cherry picked. Though it can't be manufactured, it can be channeled. It's imperative you put vehicles in place for this. But more on that later.

Ages ago, top-down marketing, the antithesis of today's desired process, was all that existed, in a formal sense. Sure, your co-worker could recommend the restaurant, movie, or soft drink that they love. But outside of that, companies were sitting atop the world concocting messages and ads and throwing them down at us. There was no social media for us to send messages upward to the masses. Big advertising was not addressing us one at a time, as individuals, trying to appeal to our senses and tastes. We were carpet bombed by commercials, billboards, and print ads as they dropped on the masses.

That model is mostly dead, or at least ineffective. We still have print and television ads, but they're not succeeding. The reason most often cited for the death of traditional advertising is the growth of technology. I suppose the DVR did put a big dent in how many people actually watch a commercial nowadays, but I'd suggest they were dying before that and it had nothing to do with recording devices.

It had everything to do with trust. We've progressed to a point where the consumer doesn't care what Carmaker A has to say about their *own* product. That consumer shopped on Amazon earlier in the day and read 42 customer testimonials and ratings about her blowdryer. She didn't even bother to look at the manufacturer's write up. Why would they now trust the television equivalent of the manufacturer's write up?

In this market, the people, from the bottom up, will choose the winners and losers. Each product in today's marketplace is a participant in this revolution. As a business owner, you will be chosen by the army in the streets and either uplifted or summarily slaughtered.

After hosting *YouShoot LIVE with Dixie Carter,* TNA's head honcho at the time, people from their camp talked to me about doing something down there. I feared they'd actually want me to hold a microphone and ask someone about winning the title, so I was a little more proactive and prepared a slideshow for TNA about what Sean Oliver *and* Kayfabe Commentaries could do for them.

They were chasing the same market that WWE owned and, quite frankly, had wrapped up pretty tightly. The market that WWE didn't have was the Internet wrestling fan, loaded with skepticism and sarcasm, waiting each week to spit out what the massive conglomerate in Connecticut was serving them. Those fans that read *The Wrestling Observer* and watched our shoot programming needed a hero—a product that spoke to them. They saw themselves as too smart for the WWE product and, on some level, they were.

The presentation I did for TNA was geared toward those fans. I pointedly told them that targeting the 11 year-old fan of John Cena was a lost cause. You'd get some spillover anyway. But designing your product to look like WWE, sound like WWE, and feature former talent of the WWE was probably a dead end.

It never really looked like it. It was not fooling anyone.

But the talent was pretty deep down in TNA and people were

watching. The federation was on the radar, so doing something cool would have been noticed and if they reached the real influencers on the Internet, its effects would have been multiplied exponentially.

Imagine if Tod Gordon and Paul Heyman had decided to try and emulate WWE's product in 1994, rather than doing everything they could to lure those that were disenfranchised, thirsting for something more real? This was that next opportunity, and I thought TNA could have the balls to grab it.

I suggested they should enter the shoot programming market, allowing us to be their conduit. If they gave us access to their roster and we produced shoots with their talent, they could use that in angles, or just to make these characters real—actually strip them of "character." They needed to target the Internet wrestling fans that were doubling and tripling in size, and we could deliver them to TNA's door. We were the biggest and best producers of shoot material in the world at the time.

Below are some of the actual slides from my July 2010 presentation to Bob Ryder and Brian Wittenstein at TNA:

KC
Kayfabe Commentaries
Presents
TOTAL NONSTOP ACTION
TNA
WRESTLING
UNCHAINED
A shoot style DVD series from the groundbreaking producers of
Guest Booker, YouShoot, and Ring Roasts.
Exploratory Discussions
July 2010
KC
Kayfabe Commentaries LLC

The Series
TNA UNCHAINED is a shoot style, DVD series, 3 or 4 releases annually. The hook is unsanctioned interview time, with no company interference.
Top talent is interviewed about their past as well as contemporary hot topics.
The show should be a source of continued soundbytes for the wrestling media to digest and syndicate, outside of the perceived "work" of a press release.
The perception of independence is the key to series success.
UNCHAINED
WHAT WOULD THEY SAY IF THEY WERE ALLOWED
KURT ANGLE
KC
Kayfabe Commentaries LLC

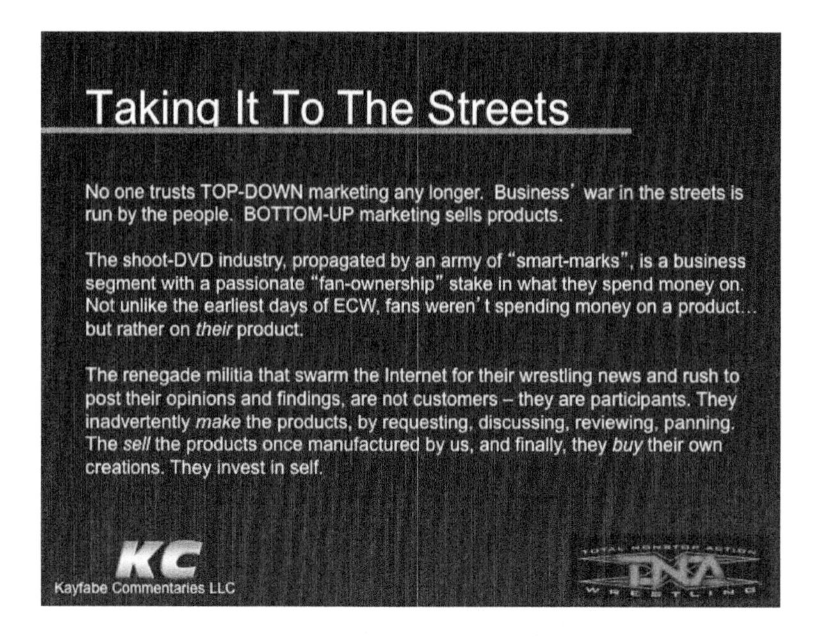

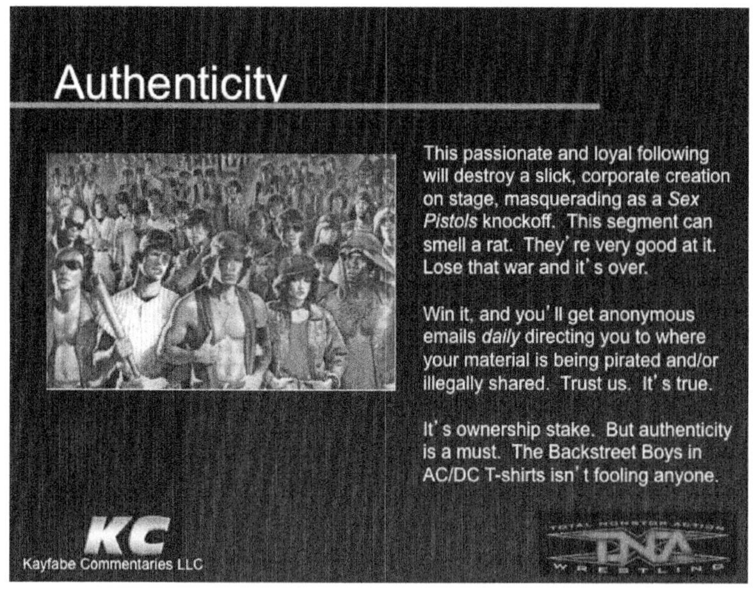

That same message was a few years ahead of its time, but I saw the importance of gathering the people and letting them do all the work. It's organic—it would have happened on its own. Beyond their graciously having me attend one of their tapings at

Universal, they never followed up. As of this writing I think their product is still on TV somewhere. I know WWE's still is.

Slick ads that only mask a flawed product will not succeed because the army in the streets gathers and communicates. Rather than clubs and bats, they're holding smartphones, and these gadgets are much more deadly for your company if you defraud their trust. A viral bludgeoning on Twitter or a slashing on Facebook can be passed on again and again, causing you to die a thousand deaths.

Conversely if you are the one placed upon their shoulders and trotted through the mean streets as the hero, you have amassed the many and the mighty who will fight for you. They are your army. You can't fool them, so don't try. They can smell your Blood.

Kayfabe Commentaries has had such a loyal allegiance with our bloodthirsty fans in the mean streets. We've found that they will literally take to the streets for us if provoked. The WWE began producing a line of high-profile products that were very similar to ours and our fans (they go so far beyond customers, it's almost an insult to refer to them a such) took great offense to this. They began showing up to WWE televised events holding up signs with our company name on it. One "Kayfabe Commando" got onto the grounds of WWE's headquarters in Stamford, Connecticut and took a photo of himself holding a big sign declaring WWE's fear of KC. We certainly don't want any of our fans to get in trouble but I'd be lying if I didn't say that kind of loyalty to our brand left me speechless and honored. We've struck a Grateful Dead-type loyalty with our viewers and it has nothing to do with the brown acid.

"Viral" has become such a buzzword today it's now worked its way into the lexicon of the big business blockheads and ad firms, always a day late in identifying cool trends. They see an ad going viral as the grand slam, but there's one component of that which is often absent. A truly viral campaign with strong brand association is a grand slam in bottom-up marketing. How often does a clever or touching ad emerge and get people talking about the commercial...but not the product? As a viewer it happens to me all the time. I can rattle off a handful of interesting commercials I've seen in the past six months and I bet I can recall maybe one or two of the products or companies they advertised.

You can be clever as all hell and win all the Obies and Cleos in the world, but if it doesn't generate sales or brand awareness for the company being advertised, you failed.

Viral ads are not awarded such status by the executive. Once again, it's the people who uplift the ads worthy of being shared, and they do that sharing on their own. It can't be manufactured. Bottom-up marketing is an organic process whose results you can't fabricate.

The mechanics are pretty simple—it really just entails social networks, blogs, podcasts, and any other ways the masses share. It's the application of these tools in concert with your brand messaging that is really the skill. If you make the tools available to your fans and you operate a genuine Business of Blood, they'll take to the streets for you too. How close to viral you get is up to them.

22. Give Them What They Want

AS YOUR PRODUCT line expands, you'll be blessed with the requests and hopes from your customers. They've been using your products and they have now formed some strong ideas about them. The access you've given them as well as the ownership stake you've instilled has made them take the time to formally address you. They've taken time out of their day, so this is clearly important to them. So in turn, we must listen.

Their opinions will vary. You'll get ten requests to make the handle blue. And then ten to make it yellow. You'll have some who feel the handle is too big, and others who think it's just right. It's pretty heavy for him, but way too light for her. They'll all let you know this, via their various opportunities to touch you...email, social nets, and otherwise.

Which of these are valid? Which do you pay attention to?

All of them. You don't have to *act* on any of them, but you do need to hear them. It's important to file these away and make note of what is being said and has been said about what you're producing, all the while being cognizant of the fact that you can't serve too many masters. But if you have a base awareness of their likes, dislikes, and suggestions, there may be a time when this will prove valuable to you.

Don't get me wrong...there are plenty of requests and comments that are dismissible from the get-go. Technology and all of these communications advances have given a voice to many who enjoy that newfound power, and look to be nothing but inflammable and negative. They post their knee jerk reactions and poorly thought-out conclusions to the world without forethought. It's pretty easy to spot them.

You need to block those out. They're not productive and they will in no way help to better your product. What they are looking for, you cannot provide, unless you have a degree in psychotherapy.

You'll become pretty good at properly categorizing customer requests after you've dealt with enough of them. Hopefully you haven't cannibalized your product too much at their direction in the meantime. You have to be able to make the distinction between *preferences* and *problems.* A customer's preferences can run the gamut. The foundations for their requests may be either thoughtful or illogical. You'll probably be able to distinguish.

If you keep reading the same thing out there, it's time to pay attention. Ask yourself some questions and be honest with the answers. Does what is being written correlate with reality? Are there conflicting comments? And most importantly—does the cash register agree?

After producing *YouShoot: LIVE* with Vince Russo, we brought him back for editions of *Guest Booker* and two *Timelines* before eventually giving him the *Vince Russo's Attitude* series. People are pretty passionate about Russo and they're very vocal with their displeasure. People posted on YouTube and on our socials about how we should be ashamed for giving him airtime. There were posts saying that people were never buying any of our shows again because we were featuring Russo on our programming.

There were lots and lots of supporters apparently, and they weren't busy posting. They were busy buying. That was their vote. And we had to listen to them. Ultimately, Vince Russo's programming became one of our top sellers.

Don't get me wrong; if the show was a deviation from our brand or we thought it wasn't servicing our fans, we wouldn't have done it in the first place. You have to ignore any post or email simply stating it was a mistake to feature Vince Russo, one of the sport's most high profile members of creative teams, most often in the head writer slot. Whether you liked what he wrote or not, his appearance on *Timeline* or *Guest Booker* is consistent with KC's brand. Sorry to those of you that don't enjoy him, but we have lots of options for you to watch other than Russo.

The late Scott Epstein was an agent/promoter type, and he grabbed me at a convention one day while we were between shoots. I'd booked occasional talent through Scott, most notably Superstar Billy Graham, and then Bruno Sammartino. That Bruno booking went a little sideways and it's in my first book *Kayfabe* so I won't rehash it all here.

I would always see Scott at the events and he was a good guy. He was a generation older than me so he had great stories of the 70s WWWF and his interactions with those guys. I liked talking to Scott and was happy to see him one night at a WSU show in Union City, NJ. WSU was an all women's federation and they were having a big show inducting some lady wrestlers into their Hall of Fame. If there's an actual Hall of Fame for WSU I'm sure it's in some garage in Brooklyn.

We were at the show working a vendor table selling our DVDs. Lisa "Ivory" Moretti was there to induct the late Luna Vachon who had died that year. I hadn't seen Moretti since we shot her edition of *Timeline* so I was happy to see her and catch up a bit. She's great—everyone in the business loves her. I saw a few other talents that I knew and I took some pictures with fans at our table. Point is, people knew I was there.

Scott Epstein came in and when it was time for the show to start, he positioned himself at a table about fifteen feet in front of us, the equivalent of two rows closer to the ring. Scott had a tiny tripod that he could clip to a little Flip camera—those were around just before every cell phone had the ability to record great quality video. I was intrigued by the little tripod and I asked if he got good video with that setup. He assured me he did, and as the show began I retuned to our table and Scott sat down at his.

He then began to construct a tower of small boxes and random objects from the venue to place his camera and baby tripod on. The thing was like six inches tall, so he had to put it atop a bunch of shit so it could shoot above the fans' heads into the ring. He then ran a cable to a laptop that he was using as a monitor to watch what the Flip was recording.

By the time Scott's production setup worthy of *Our Gang* was rolling, the ladies had assembled in the ring as Lisa Moretti eulogized Luna Vachon and inducted her into the Hall of Fame. There was a 10-bell salute and everything. As the girls talked about Luna and got emotional, I was touched.

I remembered Luna from one of our first recording sessions of our mp3 product in the early days. She wasn't one of our talent, but she attended dinner with us that night and she was sweet as pie. The chick was scary as fuck on TV, but she was so soft spoken and truthfully, probably a little zonked. I know she got sick later that night and dispatched someone to our room while we were recording with The Iron Sheik, in search of pills. Sheiky looked up and said, "What, now I am doctor?" Sheiky gives away no gimmicks, Baba.

Well, back at the arena in Union City, which was basically the size of a four-car garage, I didn't have much time to be touched by the soft-spoken induction speech in the ring. Epstein, who wore two hearing aids that were apparently malfunctioning, had turned to me and began yelling my name. He was holding his laptop up in the air and showing me, as well as everyone else, that decent video was in fact being recorded by the gimmick in which I'd expressed interest.

"Sean! Look at this, buddy! Is this beautiful or what?!"

The entire frigging place starts looking over at me and like a child I begin to slide down in my chair until I was almost under the table. Scott was oblivious to his volume during the touching in-ring eulogy. I was so embarrassed all I could do was break into a hysterical laugh. I turned and grabbed either Craig or Anthony, whoever was sitting to my left and was too big to slide under the table as well.

"Look at that video, my friend! Clear as day!"

He's still yelling, deaf as the day is long. Ivory actually pauses her speech in the ring and looks over our way, squinting to see what the commotion in the darkness was.

"Hours of video, Sean! Got a hard drive in it!"

I could stand no more. I slid out of my seat and scampered away, hanging my head and church-laughing at the mess. I ran into the restrooms for the rest of the ceremony.

Fast forward a couple of years and Epstein seeks me out at the Crowne Plaza in Monroe during the Legends of the Ring convention. He wanted a meeting with me so we met in the lobby of the hotel when I had a break and grabbed a spot on the couch. He'd never pitched me a project so I was interested in what he had. He teased me a bit when he came onto our set while we were transitioning between shows.

"I got a fortune I'm sitting on and I want you guys involved," he said to me, leaning in close like had the winning numbers. I agreed to meet him in the lobby. I was intrigued. He'd gotten so many great old timers, I wondered who he was working with for this mystery project. Hopefully it was some cool thing with Superstar Billy Graham and Bruno. Maybe Backlund too. I headed to the lobby and found Scott holding a manila envelope. We sat down.

"What do you have for me?" I asked.

"In this folder, I have all the legal paperwork to prove what I'm about to tell you." He was looking at me. Scott was an intense cat. He looked a little like Anton LaVey, founder of the church of Satan. He continued. "In about a month, I will hold the trademark for 'Hemme-sphere.' You know, as in Chirsty Hemme."

Well, it apparently wasn't going to be Bruno. I nodded along, waiting to see where this was going.

"Well, once we own the name, we can have you guys shoot her working out with a bunch of girls. You know, like yoga type stretches." He leaned in, all but salivating. "Reeeeal tight clothes."

"Okay. Then what will they do? Is it like a wrestling training video series?"

Scott pulled back, offended that he had to further explain. I guess he thought I was going to start beating off at his idea in the right there in the lobby of the Crowne Plaza beside the grand piano.

"No, that's it. It's hot chicks doing stretches in tights. You can film them from all different angles." He sat there waiting for something from me. I wasn't good at poker face that afternoon. I couldn't believe Christy was actually on board with this idea, and suspected she probably wasn't.

"That's not what we do, Scott. We're not the right guys." How did he not know? He'd seen all our stuff. I was more confused than anything else so I shook his hand and rushed back to our set to prep for the next show, which involved no hot chicks doing Downward Dog.

I know what our fans want, and I also know what they will regurgitate. You will also come to know it for your product, and you have to say 'no' when you know you won't be giving them what they want.

23. Marketzilla

EVEN AFTER HAVING carefully built your business and running it smoothly, there is one monster that can step in and sink you. Not every business is totally vulnerable to it. But those that are can do nothing to stop it. The monster is 200 feet tall and weighs a ton and a half. I'm calling it Marketzilla.

The word market is overused. In fact, it's so overused that it has come to mean so many things in business and is largely a non-word. The people that buy your product…they are your market. All of the products similar to yours make up your product market. ("We have the best widget in the entire widget market.") In a larger sense, global or national financial movements are also called markets, like the housing market or the stock market. The latter are the particular types of markets where our Marketzilla lives.

Want to stay away from the crushing feel of Marketzilla? Then the one thing you are going to avoid is starting a business that is dependent on the health of a singular market. You're giving control of your destiny away if you have made that mistake. Don't be entirely market-based.

Real estate and stocks are always referenced in close proximity to one another because they are both indicators of the financial health of a marketplace, and on a larger scale, a nation. They are also wholly market-based businesses. The success or challenges of the professional in such arenas is dictated by the performance of the outside entity we call the market. In truth, all business are affected somewhat by a market. A producer of fine, high-end cookware likely sells less during a recession and a housing slump. When there's no paycheck coming in, how many people would say, "Sweetie I was thinking, we need to upgrade our skillet to restaurant quality." And if fewer houses are selling, how many people are grabbing a set of pots for housewarming gifts? Simple enough.

The big difference in market-based businesses and business sectors on the outskirts of markets like the cookware producer is not only the ability of the cookware company to adjust, but also the inability of market-based companies to adjust. You'll hear the term market-based, but in reality we should say market-*dependent.* A real estate agency is totally market-dependent. There is no hedge, or protection, against drastic fluctuations or crises in that market. Many big real estate companies try to build additional revenue streams as a hedge—they'll start offering mortgages, doing refinances, or selling insurance. They call it one-stop shopping. The reality is, while a real estate broker's losses may be mitigated by adding ornamental services like this to the branches of the dying tree, the trunk is still rotting. The core business is still real estate. Bad market = bad performance.

At KC, we managed to thrive during an actual recession. We actually did this by doing nothing differently to adjust for the crisis. The fact that we are a Business of Blood, deeply rooted in the passions of our viewers, was insurance against turmoil. When things are good in the world, people turn to us to watch the programming they enjoy. When things are bad, guess what? They turn to their passions as well for comfort and joy. We didn't really have to adjust at all. But not all businesses will be in that position.

Let's stay with the cookware company example, under the fictional assumption that we're in a recession. The facts above remain the same as in the real estate example—our business is challenged in a recession. All consumer industries are more difficult during challenging times. If we're in a recession then people are spending less. But as a cookware company, we are in the consumer products sector, and therefore not in a market-dependent business.

The big difference between our cookware company and that real estate office is that we, as the cookware company, can make adjustments. People may not be buying or selling houses, but they will still cook and eat, despite the plummeting value of their home. We, as the cookware company, are not so closely tied to markets, or should we say we are not market-dependent. A smart move as CEO of this cookware company might be for us to start production on a line of good quality, super-inexpensive plates and silverware. Shift your product line a bit; your high-end stuff is going to move less anyway. Why fight the trend? Slow down production on the premium products, ramp up the economical alternatives for the bootstrapped consumer, and strengthen those distribution lines. Get the new stuff in the discount shopping superstores as fast as we can.

That adjustment was made possible by the fact that our company operates without market-dependence. We can make our decisions autonomously and affect our own fate. There is no Marketzilla stomping through our town, crushing our profits and holding us at his fire-breathing fate. We have options at our cookware company. The real estate broker will be selling fewer homes, at less value. That tide affects all boats. They are a pawn to the wrath and turpitude of the monster that controls them. It's easy to ride that market wave when it's heading upward. The skill required is being able to grab on and stay on for the ride.

But there's a creativity gene that gets starved in this process. Your Business of Blood allows for lots of leeway in your product lines. In addition, you're speaking to the part of the consumer that wants your product regardless of the state of the world. You're his or her escape, their joy, maybe even their vice. You'll actually be the one to survive a market apocalypse.

The real estate broker or stock trader is taking its direction from a market. They're not making changes or affecting change in any way. They're becoming versed at being a slave. It's all left-brained exercise—receive data, analyze, act. The result is eat or starve. Repeat. It's the thought process of animals and computers. Two items, not so coincidentally, which become extinct.

Part Four:

Saving It

24. Winds of Change

KAYFABE COMMENTARIES IS very much a Business of Blood. We are not market-dependent, and we have always stayed ahead in the innovation of our market segment. We've done so much correctly, it would seem we should be impervious to the trends and whims of external forces. Well, that's not the case for anyone, and it has not been the case for us.

Changes in our world and in the business models to which entertainment companies have long held, challenge us greatly. You don't always know something is dangerous until it's wrapped around your throat.

I've heard it posited that iTunes was the first crack in the surface wherein entertainment became devalued, but I don't think so. Digital delivery of content was never the enemy. Sure, iTunes began offering songs for $0.99 but there was a time when singles (45s for you old folk like me) were sold for individual songs, and after the expenses of pressing and shipping, the artist made very little. Now, there is no overhead to a single download, or very little. That hasn't changed much.

iTunes is selling entire albums (what would you call it these days?) for around $9.99 with no real overhead for those either. The consumer gets it instantly and impulse purchases are a 24-hour a day option, as no one has to worry about when the record store is closing or opening. Standing on line at the supermarket? What's that song playing overhead? Shazam it…buy it…download it. Done. I'd imagine that the music industry moved more units than before the impulse buy of a downloaded song was possible.

Piracy became a substantial threat with the introduction of Napster and later other file sharing and torrent sites. The fact of the matter is that this is a modern age plague that any entertainment company will have to deal with in some capacity. Each company has their own methods and thresholds for piracy and it's just a fact of digital life and a generational defect that most people under 40 think it's okay to steal something if it's digital and they remain anonymous. Until something happens on a larger scale and Internet service providers get in on the blockage of such activity, we will have to deal with the challenge however we can.

I don't really see piracy as the most significant blow to media either. It has greatly lowered potential sales and yes, because we have a lower ceiling on earning potential of a title, we will not spend as much on its production as we once did. But it's a fact of life for us and we're managing.

The real storm began several years ago when Netflix began sweeping through people's homes. Streaming in general has been the greatest threat to us, further fostering the notion that digital media is near worthless. The cost per program has become so infinitesimal and that is not the fault of the consumer, but the content producers ourselves. Can I really blame a customer who takes advantage of the legal option to pay $7.99 for access for 5,000 movies and TV shows? I have Netflix too.

The studios themselves have allowed their product to be offered so low by leasing programming to Netflix, Amazon Prime, and wherever else for a pittance. The entire industry could've banded together and set the cost at whatever they wanted. They could have ignored Netflix altogether, pulled their programming and made Netflix survive on the merits of only its original shows.

In entertainment, the power always rests with the content providers. Netflix, Amazon Prime, Hulu, and any other outlet airing third-party programming would cease to exist without us, the producers. So it was really our decision to offer 5,000 shows for $7.99, or $0.0016 each movie. They've made the bed and now all of us are forced to lie in it.

So in the spirit of a responsible Business of Blood, we recently launched our own subscription-based streaming network that currently airs our back catalogue and will eventually be showing premieres of new programs. This is the model that the people have demanded, and we will provide it.

But there are some realities to what the people will now be served. As a niche of a niche, we will not have the volume of subscribers that Netflix and WWE Network have, so our productions will have to scale accordingly.

This entire book has been about bobbing and weaving—stayin' alive so you can adjust and put your power into the next shot thrown. It's somewhat fitting that we close this journey with a real-time challenge and a peek inside my thinking going forward.

Our opponent is three times bigger than anything we're used to. First and foremost is the marketplace having been trained that ala carte purchases are obsolete. No one buys a movie anymore. They buy 5,000 for less than a penny each. In a niche that sells a dependable but small about of content, our content was just devalued by 1000%. Well, at least our viewer base is still as dedicated as they always were. Right?

Well, that's no longer so either. Herein lies obstacle two—the ramifications of the overabundance of shoot content via WWE Network and podcasts, crowding the marketplace. I'd always thought that would work to our advantage by mainstreaming the type of content we produce. Well, the lack of quality from many of these other sources has had the opposite effect. It anesthetized the fans. They're fed dogshit and told it's ice cream, and people won't deal with that shit for long. So they are smaller in number.

And finally, piling on the pack is the disrespect for digital media and the rampant theft and piracy. If the first two blows didn't take you out and you're hanging onto the ropes, here's an uppercut.

You have to identify the threats to your business's well being. Some will say you're whining about the state of the world. Well, no one who owns a business would say that; they will understand you are identifying the challenges. If someone asks me about our challenges at KC, I tell them. They just don't want to hear how their downloading of torrents of our shows has hurt us. They don't want to hear that expecting a company with a viewership our size to charge what Netflix does is ridiculous. We're a boutique operation working in a micro-niche, and as such we must charge more. And yeah dude, that torrent on your PC cost us. Sorry.

So let's close by addressing all three threats before we sail west, into the current. In addressing the first threat, we have launched our subscription service where you now get hundreds of hours of KC shows for a low price. We didn't choose the path of devaluing programming—that was done for us as I mentioned. But it's the reality we are in, alas our *KC Vault* subscription site. I fully expect the shows to yield a fraction of the revenue they did before. As such, I am prepared to slash production from our high of 18 new shows per year down to 4-6 at most until the model proves itself.

The second threat, overcrowding of shoot programming, is also a new reality. We've lit the way and others have arrived in the form of podcasts and WWE Network's half-assed attempts at being provocateurs. The existence of other rock bands means we just have to keep plugging in our electric guitars and hitting the road. It may be rock n roll, but they don't sound like us. I've always believed one of our moats was *us*—Anthony's writing and my on camera hosting. Competition never scared me. You can buy the guitar, but you ain't gonna sound like Eddie.

Last and least is piracy. We need help from lawmakers and the commitment from ISPs to police the Internet. I know the net-neutrality crowd will be in an uproar, but let's just stop being silly and pretending that any segment of civilized society, whether online or not, should be unregulated and free of governance against crime. You can't break the law, whether it's kiddie porn or copyright infringement. Crime is crime, and Verizon, Optimum, Cox, and whoever else is providing us with information superhighways needs to start policing them—flagging suspicious activity and shutting down the transmission of prohibited materials. They can surely code some algorithms that recognize transmission of illegal data.

It kinda sucks operating in a time period where some of the same people who laud us for providing unique programming that speaks to their Blood, would also steal our product online but never dare take anything from inside a Banana Republic or Spencers. In some way, one is crime, and the other is justified.

So just like any store with security guards or alarms at the doorway, we need to pay for anti-piracy services. Can't snag them all, but you get what you can.

Twelve years ago Kevin Sullivan walked into our hotel suite with his booking agent James Soubasis and shot an episode of this thing called *Guest Booker*. It wasn't supposed to be a series, and it wasn't even really a shoot interview. It was programming aimed at that part of Antony and me that loved hearing about the intricacies of the wrestling world, and watching a talented booker do his job. Since then we've written, shot, edited, scored, and released 175 feature-length shows.

We've been emulated, awarded, decried, and decorated. I've been the *Timeline*-guy when I'm stopped and told I've sparked some childhood love in someone. I've been the *YouShoot*-guy when I read what an asshole I come across as when asking fan questions about Batista's dick. We've watched ideas flourish and become financial successes beyond anything we'd expected back when I was sitting with Sullivan in 2007. And we've released new shows designed to revolutionize and reinvent the shoot market, only to watch them fall to the earth, and force me to put our darlings to death.

I've been complimented by some of the biggest and most respected names in the business. I've been stood-up and fucked over by its nightcrawlers. I've learned my business with no formal training, and there have been days it's made me feel invincible. And probably an equal number of days where I cannot even pick my head up to look anyone in the eye.

Your Business of Blood will be wonderful and life affirming. It will be a prison and citadel of self-doubt. Friend, it's going to be a lot, and that's why you should do it. It's like life itself—robust and full of emotion. It will make you, then break you. But you'll get up tomorrow and be made yet again.

The one thing you'll never be, is forgotten.

ABOUT THE AUTHOR

Sean Oliver is the author of the Kindle #1 Bestseller *Kayfabe,* which documents his time as co-owner of Kayfabe Commentaries, and *Fathers' Blood,* which profiles wrestling fathers.

Sean's first novel, *Sophie's Journal,* a psychological thriller, was released in 2018. He has also worked in film and television for 25 years with over a hundred credits on major motion pictures and television series.

Sean lives in New Jersey with his wife and two daughters, none of them wrestlers.

FOLLOW SEAN

Keep tabs on what he has going on in the world of both fiction and non-fiction.

WEBSITE:
http://seanoliverbooks.com/

AMAZON AUTHOR CENTRAL:
https://www.amazon.com/Sean-Oliver/e/B077P8Q8TX

BOOKBUB:
https://www.bookbub.com/authors/sean-oliver

TWITTER:
https://twitter.com/kayfabesean

Printed in Great Britain
by Amazon